A-Z Street Atlas of EDINBURGH and DISTRICT

Key to Maps

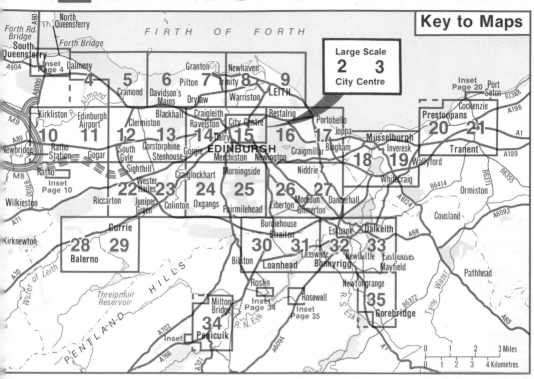

Large Scale
2 3
City Centre

FIRTH OF FORTH

Reference

Motorway	M8	Track		Ambulance Station	✚
Under Construction		Footpath		Car Park Selected	P
Road	A7	Residential Walkway		Church or Chapel	†
Under Construction		Railway	Level Crossing / Station	Fire Station	■
Road	B701	Built Up Area		Hospital	H
Dual Carriageway		District Boundary		House Numbers 'A' & 'B' Roads only	2
One-Way Street	→	Posttown Boundary By arrangement with the Post Office		Information Centre	i
Traffic flow on 'A' Roads is indicated by a heavy line on the drivers' left.		Postcode Boundary Within Posttown		National Grid Reference	³22
Pedestrianized Road				Police Station	▲
Restricted Access		Map Continuation	10 ▲ 3 ▼	Post Office	★
				Toilet / Disabled	▽ ♿
				Viewpoint	☀

Scale

1:19,000

3⅓ inches to 1 mile

0	¼	½	¾ Mile

0	0.5	1 Kilometre

Geographers' A-Z Map Co. Ltd.

Head Office : Fairfield Road, Borough Green, Sevenoaks, Kent. TN15 8PP Telephone 01732 781000

Showrooms : 44 Gray's Inn Road, Holborn, London, WC1X 8HX Telephone 0171 242 9246

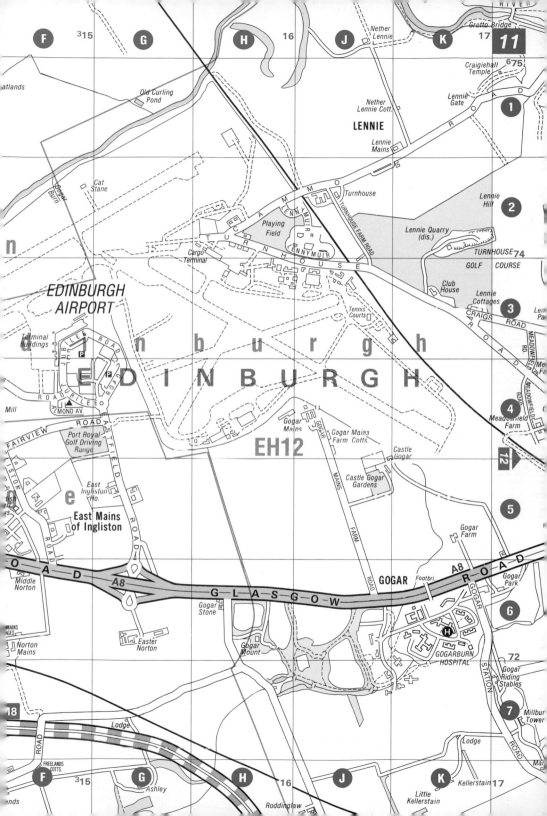

RIVER

Grotto Bridge

1

Craigiehall
Temple 675

ROAD

Nether
Lennie

Lennie
Gate

Old Curling
Pond

Nether
Lennie Cott.

LENNIE

Lennie
Mains

atlands

Cat
Stane

Turnhouse

2

Lennie
Hill

Gogar
Burn

Playing
Field

Lennie Quarry
(dis.)

TURNHOUSE 74

n

TURNHOUSE

LENNYMUIR

TURNHOUSE FARM ROAD

LENNYMUIR

Cargo
Terminal

GOLF COURSE

**EDINBURGH
AIRPORT**

Tennis
Courts

Club
House

3

Lennie
Cottages

CRAIGS ROAD

Lennie
Pa

MEADOWFIELD RD.

Terminal
Buildings

JUBILEE ROAD

ROAD

P

i n b u r g h

Mill

P

E D I N B U R G H

4

Meadowfield
Farm

MEADOWFIELD ROAD

Me
Fo

JUBILEE ROAD

AMOND AV.

12

FAIRVIEW

Port Royal
Golf Driving
Range

ROAD

Gogar
Mains

GOGAR

Gogar Mains
Farm Cotts.

Castle
Gogar

5

e

East
Ingliston
Ho.

**East Mains
of Ingliston**

EH12

Castle Gogar
Gardens

Gogar
Farm

FARM ROAD

MAINS ROAD

GLASGOW

GOGAR

Footbri.

A8

ROAD

Gogar
Park

6

Middle
Norton

A8

Gogar
Stone

**GOGARBURN
HOSPITAL**

H

GOGAR

ROAD

Easter
Norton

Gogar
Mount

Gogar
Riding
Stables

72

MAINS
GES

Norton
Mains

STATION ROAD

7

Millbur
Tower

18

Lodge

ROAD

Lodge

Mar

FREELANDS
COTTS.

Ashley

Roddinglaw

Little
Kellerstain

Kellerstain 17

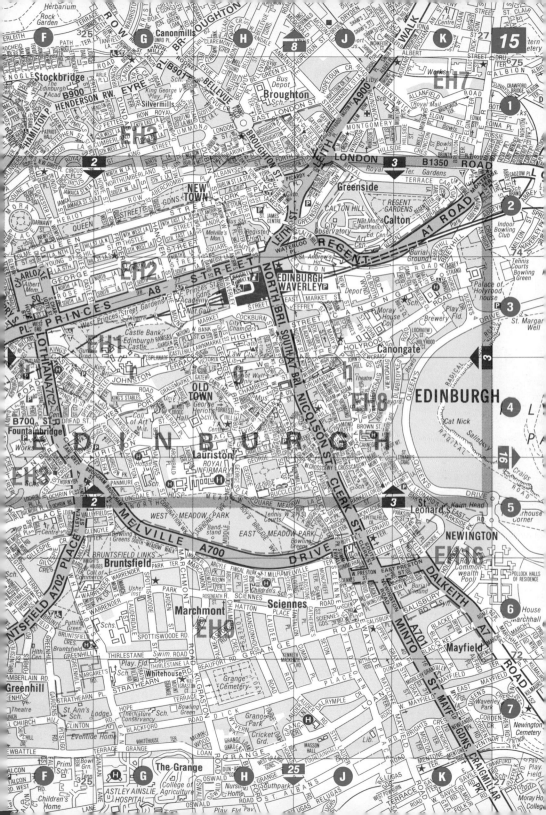

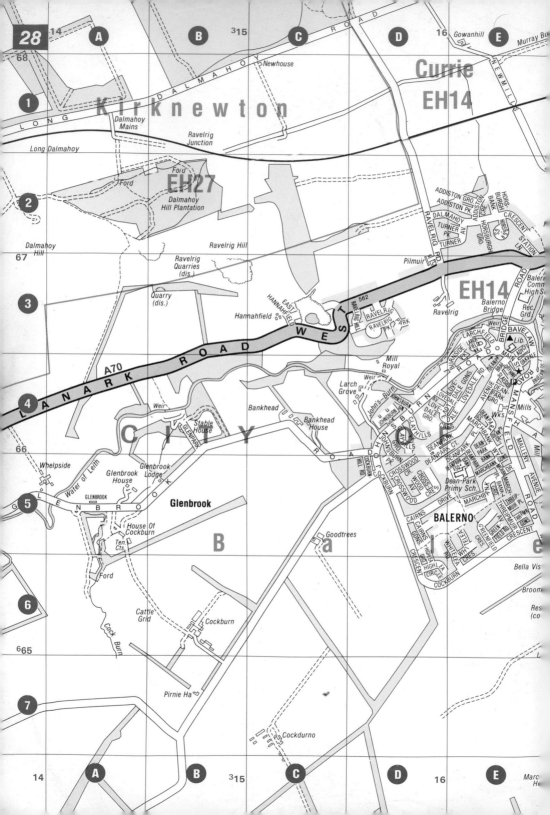

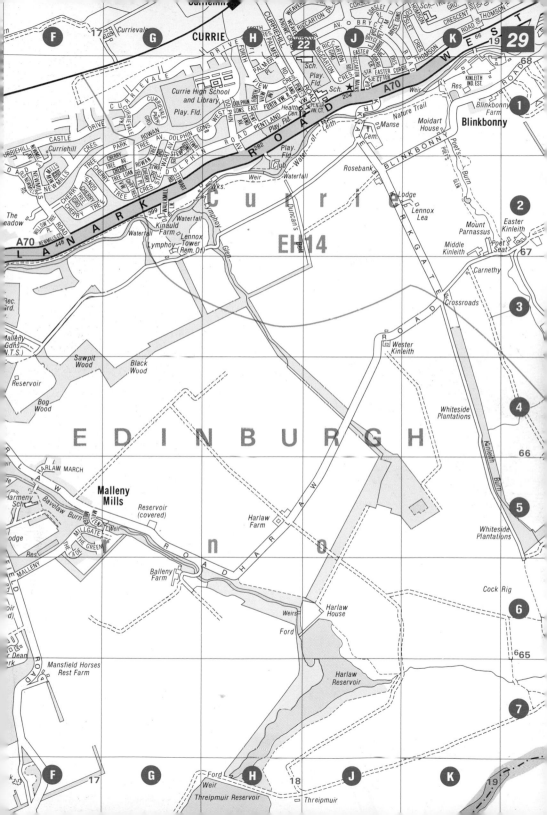

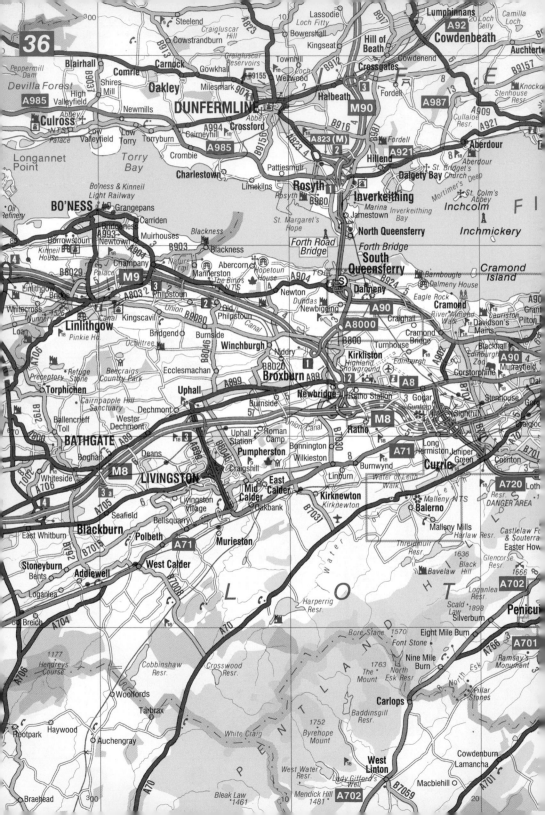

INDEX TO STREETS

HOW TO USE THIS INDEX

1. Each street name is followed by its Postal District and then by its map reference; e.g. Abbeygrange. EH22 —7F **33** is in the Edinburgh 22 Posttown and is to be found in square 7F on page **33**.
A strict alphabetical order is followed in which Av., Rd., St., etc. (though abbreviated) are read in full and as part of the street name; e.g. Ashgrove Pl. appears after Ash Gro. but before Ashgrove View.

2. Streets and a selection of Subsidiary names not shown on the Maps, appear in the index in *Italics* with the thoroughfare to which it is connected shown in brackets; e.g. *Bangholm Vs. EH5 —5B 8 (off Ferry Rd.)*

3. The page references shown in brackets indicate those streets that appear on the large scale map pages 2 and 3; e.g. Abbeyhill. EH8 —3K **15** (3K **3**) appears in square 3K on page **15** and also appears in the large scale section in square 3K on page **3**.

4. With the now general usage of Postcodes for addressing mail, it is not recommended that this index is used for such a purpose.

GENERAL ABBREVIATIONS

All: Alley	Chyd: Churchyard	Est: Estate	Mnr: Manor	S: South
App: Approach	Circ: Circle	Gdns: Gardens	Mans: Mansions	Sq: Square
Arc: Arcade	Cir: Circus	Ga: Gate	Mkt: Market	Sta: Station
Av: Avenue	Clo: Close	Gt: Great	M: Mews	St: Street
Bk: Back	Comn: Common	Grn: Green	Mt: Mount	Ter: Terrace
Boulevd: Boulevard	Cotts: Cottages	Gro: Grove	N: North	Up: Upper
Bri: Bridge	Ct: Court	Ho: House	Pal: Palace	Vs: Villas
B'way: Broadway	Cres: Crescent	Ind: Industrial	Pde: Parade	Wlk: Walk
Bldgs: Buildings	Dri: Drive	Junct: Junction	Pk: Park	W: West
Bus: Business	E: East	La: Lane	Pas: Passage	Yd: Yard
Cen: Centre	EH: Edinburgh	Lit: Little	Pl: Place	
Chu: Church	Embkmt: Embankment	Lwr: Lower	Rd: Road	

INDEX TO STREETS

Bailie Path. EH15 —5G 17
Bailie Pl. EH15 —5H 17
Bailie Ter. EH15 —5G 17
Baird Av. EH12 —5A 14
Baird Dri. EH12 —6K 13
Baird Gdns. EH12 —5A 14
Baird Gro. EH12 —5A 14
Baird Rd. EH28 —7D 10
Baird Ter. EH12 —5A 14
Bakehouse Clo. EH8 —3H 3
Balbirnie Pl. EH12 —4C 14
Balcarres Ct. EH10 —2E 24
Balcarres Pl. EH21 —1F 19
Balcarres Rd. EH21 —1F 19
Balcarres St. EH10 —2D 24
Balderston Gdns. EH16
—3B 26
Baldwin Ct. EH26 —7B 34
Balfour Ct. EH12 —2D 12
Balfour Pl. EH6 —6D 8
Balfour Sq. EH33 —6H 21
Balfour St. EH6 —6E 8
Balfour Ter. EH26 —2E 34
Balfron Loan. EH4 —2E 12
Balgreen Av. EH12 —5J 13
Balgreen Gdns. EH12 —5J 13
Balgreen Pk. EH12 —5K 13
Balgreen Rd. EH12 & EH11
—5K 13
Ballantyne La. EH6 —5E 8
Ballantyne Rd. EH6 —5E 8
Balmoral Pl. EH3 —7A 8
Balm Well Av. EH16 —7B 26
Balm Well Gro. EH16 —7B 26
Balm Well Pk. EH16 —7B 26
Balm Well Ter. EH16 —7A 26
Baltic St. EH6 —5F 9
Bangholm Av. EH5 —5A 8
Bangholm Bower Av. EH5
—5A 8
Bangholm Gro. EH5 —5B 8
Bangholm Loan. EH5 —5B 8
Bangholm Pk. EH5 —5A 8
Bangholm Pl. EH5 —5A 8
Bangholm Rd. EH5 —5A 8
Bangholm Ter. EH0 —6A 8
Bangholm View. EH5 —5B 8
Bangholm Vs. EH5 —5B 8
(off Ferry Rd.)
Bangor Rd. EH6 —5D 8
Bankhead Av. EH11 —1E 22
Bankhead B'way. EH11
—1D 22
Bankhead Cotts. EH30 —6E 4
Bankhead Crossway N. EH11
—1D 22
Bankhead Crossway S. EH11
—2D 22
Bankhead Dri. EH11 —1D 22
Bankhead Gro. EH30 —5D 4
Bankhead Ind. Est. EH12
—1E 22
Bankhead Medway. EH11
—1E 22
Bankhead Pl. EH11 —1E 22
Bankhead Rd. EH30 —5E 4
Bankhead St. EH11 —2D 22
Bankhead Ter. EH11 —2D 22
Bankhead Way. EH11 —2D 22
Bankpark Brae. EH33 —5F 21
Bankpark Cres. EH33 —5F 21
Bankpark Gro. EH33 —6C 34
Bank St. EH1 —3H 15 (4E 2)
Bank St. EH26 —7C 34
Bankton Ter. EH32 —4F 21
Barclay Pl. EH10 —5F 15
Barclay Ter. EH10 —5F 15
Barleyknowe Cres. EH23
—5H 35
Barleyknowe Gdns. EH23
—4H 35
Barleyknowe La. EH23
—5H 35
Barleyknowe Pl. EH23
—5H 35
Barleyknowe Rd. EH23
—4H 35
Barleyknowe St. EH23 —5H 35
Barleyknowe Ter. EH23
—5H 35

Barnbougle Ride. EH30 —3D 4
Barnshot Rd. EH13 —6K 23
Barntalloch Ct. EH12 —4C 12
(off Craigievar Wynd)
Barnton Av. EH4 —6K 5
Barnton Av. W. EH4 —6J 5
Barnton Brae. EH4 —6J 5
Barnton Ct. EH4 —7J 5
Barnton Gdns. EH4 —6B 6
Barntongate Av. EH4 —1D 12
Barntongate Dri. EH4 —1D 12
Barntongate Ter. EH4 —1D 12
Barnton Gro. EH4 —7J 5
Barnton Loan. EH4 —6B 6
Barnton Pk. EH4 —6B 6
Barnton Pk. Cres. EH4 —7J 5
Barnton Pk. Dell. EH4 —7A 6
Barnton Pk. Dri. EH4 —7K 5
Barnton Pk. Gdns. EH4 —7K 5
Barnton Pk. Gro. EH4 —7K 5
Barnton Pk. Pl. EH4 —7A 6
Barnton Pk. View. EH4 —7J 5
Barnton Pk. Wood. EH4
—1D 12
Barnton Roundabout. EH4
—7J 5
Barnton Ter. EH4 —2B 14
Barondale Cotts. EH22
—5F 33
Baronscourt Rd. EH8 —2C 16
Baronscourt Ter. EH8 —2D 16
Barony St. EH3 —1H 15
Barony Ter. EH12 —4F 13
Barrace Steps. EH1 —5C 2
Barracks St. EH32 —1B 20
Bathfield. EH6 —4D 8
Bath Pl. EH15 —2H 17
Bath Rd. EH6 —5G 9
Bath St. EH15 —3H 17
Bath St. La. EH15 —3H 17
Bavelaw Cres. EH26 —5A 34
Bavelaw Gdns. FH14 —4E 28
Bavelaw Rd. EH14 —3E 28
Baxter's Pl. EH1
—2J 15 (1G 3)
Bayview. EH02 —1B 20
Beach La. EH15 —3G 17
Beach La. EH21 —1F 19
Beauchamp Gro. EH16
—4A 26
Beauchamp Rd. EH16 —4A 26
Beaufort Rd. EH9 —7H 15
Beaumont Pl. EH8
—5J 15 (7H 3)
Beaverbank Pl. EH7 —7B 8
Beaverhall Rd. EH7 —7C 8
Bedford Ct. EH4 —1E 14
Bedford St. EH4 —1E 14
Bedford Ter. EH15 —3J 17
Beeches, The. EH22 —6G 33
Beech Gro. Av. EH22 —4C 32
Beechgrove Rd. EH22 —7J 33
Beech Loan. EH19 —7A 32
Beechmount Cres. EH12
—4K 13
Beechmount Pk. EH12
—5K 13
Beech Path. EH20 —6C 30
(off Niven.sknowe
Caravan Pk.)
Beech Pl. EH26 —7C 34
Beechwood Mains. EH12
—4K 13
Beechwood Pk. EH22
—7G 33
Beechwood Ter. EH6 —7G 9
Belford Av. EH4 —2C 14
Belford Bri. EH4 —3D 14
Belford Gdns. EH4 —2B 14
Belford M. EH4 —3D 14
Belford Pk. EH4 —3D 14
Belford Rd. EH4 —3D 14
Belford Ter. EH4 —3D 14
Belgrave Cres. EH4 —2D 14
Belgrave Cres. La. EH4
—2E 14
Belgrave Gdns. EH12 —4G 13
Belgrave M. EH4 —2D 14

Belgrave Pl. EH4 —2D 14
Belgrave Pl. EH12 —5G 13
Belgrave Rd. EH12 —4G 13
Belgrave Ter. EH12 —5G 13
Belhaven Pl. EH10 —2E 24
Belhaven Ter. EH10 —2E 24
Bellenden Gdns. EH16
—3C 26
Bellevue. EH7 —1H 15
Bellevue Cres. EH3 —1H 15
Bellevue Gdns. EH7 —7C 8
Bellevue Gro. EH7 —1H 15
Bellevue La. EH7 —1H 15
Bellevue Pl. EH7 —1H 15
Bellevue Rd. EH7 —1H 15
Bellevue St. EH7 —1H 15
Bellevue Ter. EH7 —1H 15
Bellfield Av. EH21 —2D 18
Bellfield Av. EH22 —3D 32
Bellfield Ct. EH21 —3D 18
Bellfield La. EH15 —3H 17
Bellfield Sq. EH32 —4C 20
Bellfield St. EH15 —3H 17
Bellfield Ter. EH15 —3H 17
Bellfield View. EH19 —5C 32
Bellmans Rd. EH26 —5B 34
Bell Pl. EH3 —1F 15
Bells Brae. EH4 —3E 14
Bell Stane. EH30 —5B 4
Bell's Wynd. EH1 —4F 3
Belmont Av. EH12 —4K 13
Belmont Cres. EH12 —4K 13
Belmont Gdns. EH12 —4K 13
Belmont Pk. EH12 —4K 13
Belmont Rd. EH14 —6E 22
Belmont Ter. EH12 —4K 13
Belmont View. EH12 —4K 13
Belvedere Pk. EH6 —4B 8
Belwood Cres. EH26 —2E 34
Belwood Rd. EH26 —2B 34
Beresford Av. EH5 —4B 8
Beresford Gdns. EH5 —5B 8
Beresford Pl. EH5 —5A 8
Beresford Ter. EH5 —5B 8
Bernard St. EH6 —4F 9
Bernard Ter. EH8 —5J 15
Beulah. EH21 —2G 19
Beulah St. EH21 —2G 19
Bevan Lee Ct. EH22 —2G 33
Bevan Rd. EH22 —1J 35
Beveridge Av. EH22 —1K 35
Beveridge Clo. EH22 —1K 35
Big Brae. EH18 —4A 32
Biggar Rd. EH10 —7F 25
Bilston Cotts. EH25 —7B 30
Bilston Glen. EH20 —6C 30
Bingham Av. EH15 —6F 17
Bingham B'way. EH15
—6F 17
Bingham Cres. EH15 —6G 17
Bingham Crossway. EH15
—6F 17
Bingham Dri. EH15 —6F 17
Bingham Medway. EH15
—6F 17
Bingham Pl. EH15 —6F 17
Bingham St. EH15 —6G 17
Bingham Way. EH15 —6F 17
Birch Ct. EH4 —1D 12
Birch Cres. EH20 —6C 30
Birkenside. EH23 —7H 35
Birnies Ct. EH4 —5D 6
Birsley Rd. EH33 —6G 21
Bishops Clo. EH1 —4F 3
Bishop's Wlk. EH3 —4E 14
Blackbarony Rd. EH16
—2A 26
Blackchapel Clo. EH15
—7H 17
Blackchapel Rd. EH15
—7H 17
Blackcot Av. EH22 —1J 35
Blackcot Dri. EH22 —1H 35
Blackcot Pl. EH22 —1J 35
Blackcot Rd. EH22 —1J 35
Blacket Av. EH9 —6K 15
Blacket Pl. EH9 —6K 15
Blackford Av. EH9 —1H 25
Blackford Bank. EH9 —1H 25
Blackford Ga. EH9 —1G 25

Blackford Glen Rd. EH16
—3J 25
Blackford Hill Gro. EH9
—2H 25
Blackford Hill Rise. EH9
—2H 25
Blackford Hill View. EH9
—2H 25
Blackford Rd. EH9 —7G 15
Blackfriars St. EH1
—3J 15 (4G 3)
Blackie Rd. EH6 —6G 9
Blackthorn Ct. EH4 —1D 12
Blackwood Cres. EH9 —6J 15
Blaeberry Gdns. EH4 —1D 12
Blair St. EH1 —3H 15 (4F 3)
Blantyre Ter. EH10 —7E 14
Blawearie Rd. EH33 —6H 21
Bleachfield. EH6 —6C 8
Blenheim Pl. EH7 —2J 15
Blenheim Pl. EH7 —1G 3
Blinkbonny Av. EH4 —2B 14
Blinkbonny Cres. EH4 —2A 14
Blinkbonny Gdns. EH4
—2B 14
Blinkbonny Gro. EH4 —2B 14
Blinkbonny Gro. W. EH4
—2B 14
Blinkbonny Rd. EH4 —2B 14
Blinkbonny Rd. EH14 —2J 29
Blinkbonny Ter. EH4 —2A 14
Boat Grn. EH3 —7B 8
Bogpark Rd. EH21 —2C 18
Bog Rd. EH26 —6B 34
Bogsmill Rd. EH14 —3K 23
Bogwood Ct. EH22 —6J 33
Bogwood Rd. EH22 —6J 33
Bonaly Av. EH13 —7J 23
Bonaly Brae. EH13 —7K 23
Bonaly Cres. EH13 —7K 23
Bonaly Dri. EH13 —7J 23
Bonaly Farm Cotts. EH13
—7J 23
Bonaly Gdns. EH13 —7J 23
Bonaly Gro. EH13 —7J 23
Bonaly Rise. EH13 —7K 23
Bonaly Rd. EH13 —6J 23
Bonaly Steading. EH13
—7J 23
Bonaly Ter. EH13 —7J 23
Bonaly Wester. EH13 —7J 23
Bonar Pl. EH6 —5C 8
Bo'ness Rd. EH30 —5A 4
Bonnington Av. EH6 —5C 8
Bonnington Gro. EH6 —5C 8
Bonnington Ind. Est. EH6
—6D 8
Bonnington Rd. EH6 —6D 8
Bonnington Rd. La. EH6
—6D 8
Bonnington Ter. EH6 —5C 8
Bonnybank Ct. EH23 —6J 35
Bonnybank Rd. EH23 —6J 35
Bonnyhaugh. EH6 —6C 8
Bonnyhaugh La. EH6 —6C 8
Bonnyrigg Rd. EH22 —4C 32
Boothacre Cotts. EH6 —6H 9
Boothacre La. EH6 —6H 9
Boroughloch La. EH8 —5J 15
Boroughloch Sq. EH8 —5J 15
Borthwick Pl. EH12 —4C 14
Borthwick's Clo. EH1 —4F 3
Boswall Av. EH5 —5J 7
Boswall Cres. EH5 —5J 7
Boswall Dri. EH5 —4J 7
Boswall Gdns. EH5 —5J 7
Boswall Grn. EH5 —5K 7
Boswall Loan. EH5 —4J 7
Boswall M. EH5 —4J 7
Boswall Parkway. EH5 —5G 7
Boswall Pl. EH5 —5J 7
Boswall Quadrant. EH5 —5J 7
Boswall Rd. EH5 —4K 7
Boswall Sq. EH5 —5J 7
Boswall Ter. EH5 —5J 7
Boswell's Clo. EH1 —4D 2
Bothwell St. EH7 —1A 16
Boundary Rd. EH14 —4A 22
Bowhill Ter. EH3 —5A 8

Bowie's Clo. EH6 —5F 9
Bowling Grn. Rd. EH29
—2B 10
Bowling Grn., The. EH6 —5E 8
Bowling La. EH6 —5E 8
(off Bowling Grn., The.)
Boyd-Orr Dri. EH26 —3C 34
Boyd's Entry. EH1
—3J 15 (4G 3)
Boy's Brigade Wlk. EH3
—5H 15 (7E 2)
Braefoot Ter. EH16 —3A 26
Braehead Av. EH4 —7H 5
Braehead Bank. EH4 —7H 5
Braehead Cres. EH4 —7H 5
Braehead Dri. EH4 —7H 5
Braehead Gro. EH4 —7H 5
Braehead Loan. EH4 —7H 5
Braehead Pk. EH4 —7H 5
Braehead Rd. EH4 —7H 5
Braehead Row. EH4 —7H 5
Braehead View. EH4 —7H 5
Brae Pk. EH4 —6H 5
Brae Pk. Rd. EH4 —7H 5
Braeside Rd. EH20 —5G 31
Braeside Rd. N. EH23 —6J 35
Braeside Rd. S. EH23 —6J 35
Braid Av. EH10 —3F 25
Braidburn Cres. EH10 —3E 24
Braidburn Ter. EH10 —3E 24
Braid Cres. EH10 —3E 24
Braid Farm Rd. EH10 —3E 24
Braid Hills App. EH10 —4F 25
Braid Hills Av. EH10 —3E 24
Braid Hills Cres. EH10
—4E 24
Braid Hills Dri. EH10 & EH16
—3G 25
Braid Hills Rd. EH10 —4E 24
Braidlaw Rd. EH26 —7A 34
Braid Mt. EH10 —4E 24
Braid Mt. Crest. EH10 —4F 25
Braid Mt. Rise. EH10 —4F 25
Braid Mt. View. EH10 —4F 25
Braid Rd. EH10 —3E 24
Bramble Dri. EH4 —1D 12
Bramdean Gro. EH10 —4F 25
Bramdean Pl. EH10 —4F 25
Bramdean Rise. EH10 —4F 25
Bramdean View. EH10 —4F 25
Brand Dri. EH15 —5H 17
Brandfield St. EH3 —5E 14
Brand Gdns. EH15 —4J 17
Brandon St. EH3 —1G 15
Brandon Ter. EH3 —1G 15
Brand Pl. EH8 —2A 16
Breadalbane St. EH6 —5D 8
Breadalbane Ter. EH11
—4E 14
Bread St. EH3 —4F 15 (6B 2)
Bread St. S. La. EH3 —6B 2
Breck Ter. EH26 —3D 34
Breidwood Ga. EH8
—4J 15 (6H 3)
Brewers Bush. EH9 —3F 35
Brewery Clo. EH30 —5B 4
Brewery La. EH6 —5E 8
Briarbank Ter. EH11 —7C 14
Brickfield. EH15 —2G 17
Brickworks Rd. EH33 —5F 21
Bridgend. EH22 —1E 32
Bridgend Ct. EH22 —2F 33
(off Edinburgh Rd.)
Bridge Pl. EH3 —1E 14
Bridge Rd. EH13 —6J 23
Bridge Rd. EH14 —3E 28
Bridge St. EH15 —2G 17
Bridge St. EH21 —2E 18
Bridge St. EH26 —7C 34
Bridge St. EH28 —5A 10
Bridge St. EH33 —6G 21
Bridge St. La. EH15 —2G 17
Briery Bauks. EH8
—4J 15 (6H 3)
Brighton Cres. EH15 —3G 17
Brighton Pl. EH15 —3G 17
Brighton St. EH1
—4H 15 (5F 3)
Brights Cres. EH9 —7K 15
Bright Ter. EH11 —4E 14

Carlowrie Av. EH30 —7E **4**
Carlowrie Cres. EH30 —7E **4**
Carlowrie Pl. EH23 —5J **35**
Carlton St. EH4 —2E **14**
Carlton Ter. EH7
   —2K **15** (1K **3**)
Carlton Ter. Brae. EH7
   —2K **15** (1K **3**)
Carlton Ter. La. EH7
   —2K **15** (1J **3**)
Carlton Ter. M. EH7
   —2K **15** (1J **3**)
Carlyle Pl. EH21 —2E **18**
Carmel Av. EH29 —1A **10**
Carmelite Rd. EH30 —6B **4**
Carmel Rd. EH29 —2A **10**
Carnegie Ct. EH8 —6H **3**
Carnegie St. EH8
   —4J **15** (6H **3**)
Carnethie St. EH24 —7F **35**
Carnethy Av. EH13 —7J **23**
Carnethy Av. EH26 —5C **34**
Carnethy Ct. EH26 —6C **34**
Caroline Gdns. EH12 —4G **13**
Caroline Pk. Av. EH5 —3G **7**
Caroline Pk. Gro. EH5 —4G **7**
Caroline Pl. EH12 —4G **13**
Caroline Ter. EH12 —3E **12**
Carpet La. EH6 —5F **9**
Carrick Cres. EH22 —5H **33**
Carrick Knowe Av. EH12
   —5H **13**
Carrick Knowe Dri. EH12
   —6G **13**
Carrick Knowe Gdns. EH12
   —6H **13**
Carrick Knowe Gro. EH12
   —6H **13**
Carrick Knowe Hill. EH12
   —6H **13**
Carrick Knowe Loan. EH12
   —6G **13**
Carrick Knowe Parkway. EH12
   —6G **13**
Carrick Knowe Pl. EH12
   —6H **13**
Carrick Knowe Rd. EH12
   —7G **13**
Carrick Knowe Ter. EH12
   —6H **13**
Carrington Cres. EH4 —7H **7**
Carrington Ho. EH4 —7H **7**
Carrington Rd. EH4 —1C **14**
Carron Pl. EH6 —5G **9**
Carruber's Clo. EH1 —4F **3**
Casselbank St. EH6 —6E **8**
Cassel's La. EH6 —6E **8**
Castle Av. EH12 —6F **13**
Castle Av. EH32 —1C **20**
Castlebarns Steps. EH1 —5B **2**
Castlehill. EH1 —3G **15** (4D **2**)
Castlelaw Cres. EH25 —7B **30**
Castlelaw Rd. EH13 —6J **23**
Castle Rd. EH32 —1C **20**
Castle Rd. EH33 —7F **21**
Castle St. EH2 —3F **15** (3B **2**)
Castle Ter. EH1 —4F **15** (4B **2**)
Castle Ter. EH32 —1C **20**
Castle View. EH32 —1C **20**
Castleview Ho. EH17 —4D **26**
Castle Wlk. EH32 —1C **20**
Castle Wynd N. EH1 —5D **2**
Castle Wynd S. EH1 —5D **2**
Cast, The. EH18 —7H **31**
Cathcart Pl. EH11 —5D **14**
Catherine Pl. EH3 —7B **8**
Catriona Ter. EH26 —2E **34**
Cauldcoats Cotts. EH22
   —2H **27**
Causewayside. EH9 —6J **15**
Causeway, The. EH15 —5C **16**
Cavalry Pk. Dri. EH15 —5D **16**
Cedar Dri. EH32 —1G **21**
Cedar Rd. EH20 —6B **30**
Cedars, The. EH13 —5K **23**
Cemetery Rd. EH22 —3E **32**
Cemetery Rd. EH32 —2D **20**
Chalmers Bldgs. EH3 —7A **2**
Chalmer's Clo. EH1 —4G **3**

Chalmers Cres. EH9 —6H **15**
Chalmers St. EH3
   —4G **15** (6D **2**)
Chamberlain Rd. EH10
   —7F **15**
Chambers St. EH1
   —4H **15** (5E **2**)
Champigny Ct. EH21 —3G **19**
Chancelot Cres. EH5 —5B **8**
Chancelot Gro. EH5 —5B **8**
Chancelot Ter. EH6 —5B **8**
Chapel Ct. EH16 —7E **16**
Chapel Ga. Rd. EH30 —2A **4**
Chapel La. EH1 —2H **15** (1F **3**)
Chapel La. EH6 —5F **9**
Chapel Loan. EH25 —1B **34**
Chapel St. EH8 —5J **15** (6G **3**)
Chapel Wynd. EH1 —5C **2**
Charlesfield. EH8
   —4H **15** (6F **3**)
Charles St. EH8 —4H **15** (6F **3**)
Charles St. EH26 —4B **34**
Charles St. La. EH8
   —4H **15** (6F **3**)
Charlotte La. EH2
   —3F **15** (3A **2**)
Charlotte Sq. EH2
   —3F **15** (3A **2**)
Charlton Gro. EH25 —1A **34**
Charterhall Gro. EH9 —1H **25**
Charterhall Rd. EH9 —2H **25**
Cherry La. EH22 —/K **33**
Cherry Rd. EH19 —7A **32**
Cherry Tree Av. EH14 —2G **29**
Cherry Tree Cres. EH14
   —2F **29**
Cherry Tree Gdns. EH14
   —2F **29**
Cherry Tree Gro. EH14
   —2F **29**
Cherry Tree Loan. EH14
   —2G **29**
Cherry Tree Pk. EH14 —2F **29**
Cherry Tree Pl. EH14 —2G **29**
Cherry Tree View. EH14
   —2G **29**
Chessel's Clo. EH8 —4G **3**
Chessel's Ct. EH8 —3J **15**
Chesser Av. EH14 —7K **13**
Chesser Cotts. EH11 —7A **14**
Chesser Cres. EH14 —1K **23**
Chesser Gdns. EH14 —7K **13**
Chesser Gro. EH14 —1K **23**
Chesser Ho. EH11 —7K **13**
Chesser Loan. EH14 —1K **23**
Chester Ct. EH19 —7A **32**
Chester Dri. EH22 —1J **35**
Chester Gro. EH19 —7A **32**
Chester St. EH3 —3E **14**
Chesters View. EH19 —7A **32**
Chestnut Gro. EH19 —7A **32**
Chestnut St. EH5 —3H **7**
Cheyne St. EH4 —1E **14**
Chisholm St. EH26 —4C **34**
Christian Cres. EH15 —4H **17**
Christian Gro. EH15 —4H **17**
Christian Path. EH15 —1G **17**
Christiemiller Av. EH7 —1E **16**
Christiemiller Gro. EH7
   —2E **16**
Christiemiller Pl. EH7 —2E **16**
Chuckie Pend. EH3
   —4F **15** (6A **2**)
Church Hill. EH10 —7F **15**
Church Hill Pl. EH10 —7F **15**
Churchill Dri. EH10 —7F **15**
Church La. EH21 —3E **18**
Church Rd. EH14 —4J **31**
Church St. EH20 —6F **31**
Church St. EH33 —5G **21**
Circle, The. EH22 —4H **27**
Circus Gdns. EH3
   —2F **15** (1B **2**)
Circus La. EH3 —1F **15** (1B **2**)
Circus Pl. EH3 —2F **15** (1B **2**)
*Citadel Ct. EH6 —4E **8***
(off Couper St.)
Citadel Pl. EH6 —4E **8**
Citadel St. EH6 —4E **8**

City of Edinburgh By-Pass,
   The. EH12 & EH21 —6B **12**
Civic Sq. EH33 —6H **21**
Clackmae Gro. EH16 —4K **25**
Clackmae Rd. EH16 —4K **25**
Clapper La. EH16 —2A **26**
Clarebank Cres. EH6 —6G **9**
Claremont Bank. EH7 —1H **15**
Claremont Ct. EH7 —7C **8**
Claremont Cres. EH7 —7C **8**
Claremont Gdns. EH6 —6H **9**
Claremont Gro. EH7 —7C **8**
Claremont Pk. EH6 —6G **9**
Claremont Rd. EH6 —6G **9**
Clarence St. EH3 —1F **15**
Clarendon Cres. EH4 —2E **14**
Clarinda Gdns. EH22 —3J **33**
Clarinda Ter. EH16 —4A **26**
Clark Av. EH5 —5B **8**
Clark Pl. EH5 —5A **8**
Clark Rd. EH5 —5A **8**
Claverhouse Dri. EH16
   —4A **26**
Clayhills Gro. EH14 —4D **28**
Clayhills Pk. EH14 —4D **28**
Clayknowes Av. EH21 —4C **18**
Clayknowes Ct. EH21 —4C **18**
Clayknowes Dri. EH21 —4C **18**
Clayknowes Pl. EH21 —3C **18**
Clayknowes Rd. EH21 —3C **18**
Clayknowes Way. EH21
   —3C **18**
Clearburn Cres. EH16 —7B **16**
Clearburn Gdns. EH16 —7B **16**
Clearburn Rd. EH16 —7B **16**
Clearburn Rd. EH23 —4G **35**
Cleekim Dri. EH15 —7H **17**
Cleekim Rd. EH15 —7H **17**
Cleikiminfield. EH15 —7H **17**
Cleikiminrig. EH15 —7H **17**
Cleric's Hill. EH29 —2A **10**
Clerk Rd. EH26 — 6A **34**
Clerk St. EH8 —5J **15** (7G **3**)
Clerk St. EH20 —5F **31**
Clermiston Av. EH4 —1F **13**
Clermiston Cres. EH4 —1F **13**
Clermiston Dri. EH4 —2F **13**
Clermiston Gdns. EH4 —2F **13**
Clermiston Grn. EH4 —1F **13**
Clermiston Gro. EH4 —2F **13**
Clermiston Hill. EH4 —1F **13**
Clermiston Junction. EH4
   —7B **6**
Clermiston Loan. EH4 —1F **13**
Clermiston Medway. EH4
   —1F **13**
Clermiston Pk. EH4 —1F **13**
Clermiston Pl. EH4 —2F **13**
Clermiston Rd. EH12 —4G **13**
Clermiston Rd. N. EH4
   —1G **13**
Clermiston Ter. EH12 —4G **13**
Clermiston View. EH4 —1G **13**
Clerwood Bank. EH12 —3F **13**
Clerwood Gdns. EH12 —3F **13**
Clerwood Gro. EH12 —3G **13**
Clerwood Loan. EH12 —3F **13**
Clerwood Pk. EH12 —3F **13**
Clerwood Pl. EH12 —3G **13**
Clerwood Row. EH12 —3F **13**
Clerwood Ter. EH12 —3G **13**
Clerwood View. EH12 —3G **13**
Clerwood Way. EH12 —3F **13**
Clifton Hall Rd. EH28 —6A **10**
Clifton Ter. EH12 —4E **14**
Clinton Rd. EH9 —7F **15**
Clockmill La. EH8 & EH7
   —2B **16**
Close, The. EH30 —6A **4**
Clove Cottage. EH12 —2A **22**
Clovenstone Dri. EH14
   —5G **23**
Clovenstone Gdns. EH14
   —4G **23**
Clovenstone Pk. EH14 —5G **23**
Clovenstone Rd. EH14
   —4G **23**
Cluny Av. EH10 —2F **25**
Cluny Dri. EH10 —2F **25**
Cluny Gdns. EH10 —2F **25**

Cluny Pl. EH10 —1G **25**
Cluny Ter. EH10 —1F **25**
Clyde St. EH1 —2H **15** (2E **2**)
Coalgate Av. EH33 —5J **21**
Coalgate Rd. EH33 —5H **21**
Coalhill. EH6 —5E **8**
Coal Neuk. EH33 —6G **21**
Coates Cres. EH3 —4E **14**
Coates Gdns. EH12 —4D **14**
Coates Pl. EH3 —4E **14**
Coatfield La. EH6 —5F **9**
Cobbinshaw Ho. EH11 —3E **22**
Cobden Cres. EH9 —7K **15**
Cobden Rd. EH9 —7K **15**
Cobden Ter. EH11 —4E **14**
Cockburn Cres. EH14 —5D **28**
Cockburnhill Rd. EH14
   —5D **28**
Cockburn St. EH1
   —3H **15** (4E **2**)
Cockmylane. EH13 —5D **24**
Cockpen Av. EH19 —7K **31**
Cockpen Cres. EH19 —7K **31**
Cockpen Dri. EH19 —7K **31**
Cockpen Pl. EH19 —7K **31**
Cockpen Rd. EH19 —7B **32**
Cockpen Ter. EH19 —7K **31**
Cockpen View. EH19 —7K **31**
Coffin La. EH11 —5D **14**
Coillesdene Av. EH15 —4K **17**
Coillesdene Cres. EH15
   —4K **17**
Coillesdene Dri. EH15 —4K **17**
Coillesdene Gdns. EH15
   —4K **17**
Coillesdene Gro. EH15
   —4K **17**
Coillesdene Ho. EH15 —4K **17**
Coillesdene Loan. EH15
   —1A **18**
Coillesdene Ter. EH15 —4K **17**
Colinyie Ho. Clo. EH1 —4G **3**
Colinton Gro. EH14 —2B **24**
Colinton Gro. W. EH14
   —2B **24**
Colinton Mains Cres. EH13
   —6C **24**
Colinton Mains Dri. EH13
   —4B **24**
Colinton Mains Gdns. EH13
   —4B **24**
Colinton Mains Grn. EH13
   —5B **24**
Colinton Mains Gro. EH13
   —5C **24**
Colinton Mains Loan. EH13
   —5B **24**
Colinton Mains Pl. EH13
   —5C **24**
Colinton Mains Rd. EH13
   —5B **24**
Colinton Mains Ter. EH13
   —5C **24**
Colinton Rd. EH10 —1C **24**
Colinton Rd. EH13 & EH14
   —5K **23**
College Wynd. EH1 —5F **3**
Collins Pl. EH3 —1F **15**
Colmestone Ga. EH10 —6E **24**
Coltbridge Av. EH12 —4B **14**
Coltbridge Gdns. EH12
   —3C **14**
Coltbridge Ter. EH12 —4B **14**
Coltbridge Vale. EH12 —4C **14**
Columba Av. EH4 —1K **13**
Columba Rd. EH4 —1K **13**
Colville Pl. EH3 —1F **15**
Comely Bank. EH4 —1D **14**
Comely Bank Av. EH4 —1E **14**
Comely Bank Gro. EH4
   —1D **14**
Comely Bank Pl. EH4 —1E **14**
Comely Bank Pl. M. EH4
   —1E **14**
Comely Bank Rd. EH4
   —1E **14**

Comely Bank Row. EH4
   —1E **14**
Comely Bank St. EH4 —1D **14**
Comely Bank Ter. EH4 —1E **14**
Comely Grn. Cres. EH7
   —2A **16**
Comely Grn. Pl. EH7 —2A **16**
Comiston Dri. EH10 —3D **24**
Comiston Gdns. EH10 —2E **24**
Comiston Gro. EH10 —5E **24**
Comiston Pl. EH10 —2E **24**
Comiston Rise. EH10 —5E **24**
Comiston Rd. EH10 —4E **24**
Comiston Springs Av. EH10
   —5E **24**
Comiston Ter. EH10 —2E **24**
Comiston View. EH10 —5E **24**
Commercial St. EH6 —4E **8**
Commercial Wharf. EH6
   —4F **9**
Conifer Rd. EH22 —6K **33**
Connaught Pl. EH6 —5C **8**
Considene Gdns. EH8 —2C **16**
Considene Ter. EH8 —2C **16**
Constitution Pl. EH6 —4F **9**
Constitution St. EH6 —6F **9**
Cook Cres. EH22 —1J **35**
*Cookies Wynd. EH32 —3C **20***
(off Rope Wlk.)
Co-operative Bldgs. EH33
   —6H **21**
Cope La. EH32 —1B **20**
Corbiehill Av. EH4 —7D **6**
Corbiehill Cres. EH4 —5C **6**
Corbiehill Gdns. EH4 —7D **6**
Corbiehill Gro. EH4 —7D **6**
Corbiehill Pk. EH4 —7C **6**
Corbiehill Pl. EH4 —7C **6**
Corbiehill Rd. EH4 —7C **6**
Corbiehill Ter. EH4 —7C **6**
Corbieshot. EH15 —6H **17**
Cornhill Ter. EH6 —6G **9**
Cornwallis Pl. EH3 —1G **15**
Cornwall St. EH1
   —4F **15** (5B **2**)
Cornation Pl. EH22 —6J **33**
Coronation Pl. EH33 —6G **21**
Coronation Wlk. EH3
   —5G **15** (7D **2**)
Corrennie Dri. EH10 —2F **25**
Corrennie Gdns. EH10 —3F **25**
Corrie Ct. EH22 —2G **35**
Corslet Cres. EH14 —7D **22**
Corslet Pl. EH14 —7C **22**
Corslet Rd. EH14 —7C **22**
Corstorphine Bank Av.
   —4E **12**
Corstorphine Bank Dri.
   —4E **12**
Corstorphine Bank Ter.
   —4E **12**
Corstorphine High St. EH12
   —5F **13**
Corstorphine Hill Av. EH12
   —4G **13**
Corstorphine Hill Cres. EH12
   —4G **13**
Corstorphine Hill Gdns. EH12
   —4G **13**
Corstorphine Hill Rd. EH12
   —4G **13**
Corstorphine Ho. Av. EH12
   —5G **13**
Corstorphine Ho. Ter. EH12
   —5G **13**
Corstorphine Pk. Gdns. EH12
   —5G **13**
Corstorphine Rd. EH12
   —5H **13**
Cortleferry Dri. EH22 —4D **32**
Cortleferry Gro. EH22 —4D **32**
Cortleferry Pk. EH22 —4D **32**
Cortleferry Ter. EH22 —4D **32**
Corunna Pl. EH6 —5E **8**
Corunna Ter. EH26 —3D **34**
Cotlaws. EH29 —2A **10**
Cottage Grn. EH4 —6J **5**
Cottage Homes. EH13 —6K **23**
Cottage La. EH21 —3G **19**
Cottage Pk. EH4 —2J **13**

County Rd. EH32 —3C **20**
County Sq. EH32 —3C **20**
Couper St. EH6 —4E **8**
Cowan Rd. EH11 —7C **14**
Cowan's Clo. EH8
—5J **15** (7H 3)
Cowan Ter. EH26 —4C **34**
Cowden Cres. EH22 —2J **33**
Cowden Gro. EH22 —2J **33**
Cowden La. EH22 —2J **33**
Cowden Pk. EH22 —2H **33**
Cowden Ter. EH22 —2J **33**
Cowden View. EH22 —2J **33**
Cowgate. EH1 —4H **15** (5E **2**)
Cowgatehead. EH1
—4H **15** (5E **2**)
Cowpits. EH21 —6F **19**
Cowpits Rd. EH21 —5E **18**
(Monktonhall)
Cowpits Rd. EH21 —6F **19**
(Whitecraig)
Coxfield. EH11 —6B **14**
Craigcrook Av. EH4 —1H **13**
Craigcrook Gdns. EH4 —2K **13**
Craigcrook Gro. EH4 —2J **13**
Craigcrook Pk. EH4 —2J **13**
Craigcrook Pl. EH4 —2A **14**
Craigcrook Rd. EH4 —7C **6**
Craigcrook Sq. EH4 —2G **9**
Craigcrook Ter. EH4 —1A **14**
Craigend Pk. EH16 —3C **26**
Craigentinny Av. EH7 —1D **16**
Craigentinny Av. N. EH6
—6J **9**
Craigentinny Cres. EH7
—2E **16**
Craigentinny Gro. EH7 —2E **16**
Craigentinny Pl. EH7 —2E **16**
Craigentinny Rd. EH7 —2E **16**
Craighall Av. EH6 —4B **8**
Craighall Bank. EH6 —5C **8**
Craighall Cres. EH6 —4B **8**
Craighall Gdns. EH6 —5B **8**
Craighall Rd. EH6 —4B **8**
Craighall Ter. EH6 —5B **8**
Craighall Ter. EH21 —2H **19**
Craighill Gdns. EH10 —3D **24**
Craighouse Av. EH10 —2D **24**
Craighouse Gdns. EH10
—2D **24**
Craighouse Pk. EH10 —2D **24**
Craighouse Rd. EH10 —2D **24**
Craighouse Ter. EH10 —2D **24**
Craigiebield Cres. EH26
—7B **34**
Craigievar Pk. EH12 —3D **12**
Craigievar Sq. EH12 —3C **12**
Craigievar Wynd. EH12
—4C **12**
Craiglea Dri. EH10 —3D **24**
Craiglea Pl. EH10 —3D **24**
Craigleith Av. N. EH4 —3A **14**
Craigleith Av. S. EH4 —3A **14**
Craigleith Bank. EH4 —2B **14**
Craigleith Cres. EH4 —2A **14**
Craigleith Dri. EH4 —2A **14**
Craigleith Gdns. EH4 —2A **14**
Craigleith Gro. EH4 —2A **14**
Craigleith Hill. EH4 —2B **14**
Craigleith Hill Av. EH4 —1B **14**
Craigleith Hill Cres. EH4
—1B **14**
Craigleith Hill Gdns. EH4
—1B **14**
Craigleith Hill Grn. EH4
—1B **14**
Craigleith Hill Gro. EH4
—1B **14**
Craigleith Hill Loan. EH4
—1B **14**
Craigleith Hill Pk. EH4 —1B **14**
Craigleith Hill Row. EH4
—1B **14**
Craigleith Rise. EH4 —3A **14**
Craigleith Rd. EH4 —2B **14**
Craigleith Trading Est. EH4
—1B **14**
Craigleith View. EH4 —3A **14**
Craiglockhart Av. EH14
—2A **24**

Craiglockhart Bank. EH14
—3A **24**
Craiglockhart Cres. EH14
—3A **24**
Craiglockhart Dell Rd. EH14
—2A **24**
Craiglockhart Dri. N. EH14
—2B **24**
Craiglockhart Dri. S. EH14
—4A **24**
Craiglockhart Gdns. EH14
—2A **24**
Craiglockhart Gro. EH14
—4A **24**
Craiglockhart Loan. EH14
—3A **24**
Craiglockhart Pk. EH14
—3A **24**
Craiglockhart Pl. EH14
—2B **24**
Craiglockhart Quadrant. EH14
—3A **24**
Craiglockhart Rd. EH14
—4A **24**
Craiglockhart Rd. N. EH14
—3B **24**
Craiglockhart Ter. EH14
—2C **24**
Craiglockhart View. EH14
—2B **24**
Craigmillar Castle Av. EH16
—1D **26**
Craigmillar Castle Gdns. EH16
—7D **16**
Craigmillar Castle Gro. EH16
—7D **16**
Craigmillar Castle Loan. EH16
—7E **16**
Craigmillar Castle Rd. EH16
—7D **16**
Craigmillar Castle Ter. EH16
—1D **26**
Craigmillar Ct. EH16 —1C **26**
Craigmillar Pk. EH16 —1K **25**
Craigmount App. EH12
—4E **12**
Craigmount Av. EH12 —4E **12**
Craigmount Av. N. EH4 & EH12
—2D **12**
Craigmount Bank. EH4
—2D **12**
Craigmount Bank W. EH4
—2D **12**
Craigmount Brae. EH12
—2D **12**
Craigmount Ct. EH4 —2D **12**
Craigmount Cres. EH12
—3D **12**
Craigmount Dri. EH12 —3D **12**
Craigmount Gdns. EH12
—4D **12**
Craigmount Gro. EH12
—4D **12**
Craigmount Gro. N. EH12
—3D **12**
Craigmount Hill. EH4 —2D **12**
Craigmount Loan. EH12
—3D **12**
Craigmount Pk. EH12 —4D **12**
Craigmount Pl. EH12 —3D **12**
Craigmount Ter. EH12
—4D **12**
Craigmount View. EH12
—3D **12**
Craigmount Way. EH12
—2E **12**
Craigour Av. EH17 —4E **26**
Craigour Cotts. EH17 —4E **26**
Craigour Cres. EH17 —4E **26**
Craigour Dri. EH17 —3D **26**
Craigour Gdns. EH17 —4E **26**
Craigour Grn. EH17 —4D **26**
Craigour Gro. EH17 —4E **26**
Craigour Loan. EH17 —4E **26**
Craigour Pl. EH17 —4D **26**
Craigour Ter. EH17 —4E **26**
Craigpark. EH28 —7A **10**
Craigpark Cres. EH28 —7A **10**
Craigs Av. EH12 —5D **12**
Craigs Bank. EH12 —4D **12**

Craig's Clo. EH1 —4F **3**
Craigs Cres. EH12 —4D **12**
Craigs Dri. EH12 —4D **12**
Craigs Gdns. EH12 —4D **12**
Craigs Gro. EH12 —5E **12**
Craigs Loan. EH12 —4E **12**
(in two parts)
Craigs Pk. EH12 —4D **12**
Craigs Rd. EH12 —3K **11**
Crame Ter. EH22 —3D **32**
Cramond Av. EH4 —4J **5**
Cramond Bank. EH4 —5J **5**
Cramond Bri. Cotts. EH4
—6G **5**
Cramond Brig Toll. EH4
—6G **5**
Cramond Cres. EH4 —5J **5**
Cramond Gdns. EH4 —5J **5**
Cramond Glebe Gdns. EH4
—4K **5**
Cramond Glebe Rd. EH4
—4J **5**
Cramond Glebe Ter. EH4
—4J **5**
Cramond Grn. EH4 —4J **5**
(in two parts)
Cramond Gro. EH4 —5J **5**
Cramond Pk. EH4 —5J **5**
Cramond Pl. EH4 —5K **5**
Cramond Regis. EH4 —6J **5**
Cramond Rd. N. EH4 —4K **5**
Cramond Rd. S. EH4 —5A **6**
Cramond Ter. EH4 —5J **5**
Cramond Vale. EH4 —5H **5**
Cramond Village. EH4 —3J **5**
Cranston St. EH8
—3J **15** (3G **3**)
Cranston St. EH26 —6B **34**
Crarae Av. EH4 —3B **14**
Craufurdland. EH4 —7H **5**
Crawford Bri. EH7 —1A **16**
Crawfurd Rd. EH16 —1A **26**
Crawlees Cres. EH22 —7K **33**
Crawlees of Smithy Cotts.
EH22 —2H **35**
Crawlees Rd. EH23 & EH22
—3G **35**
Crawley Cotts. EH26 —1C **34**
Crescent, The. EH10 —2E **24**
Crescent, The. EH23 —3H **35**
Crewe Bank. EH5 —5H **7**
Crewe Cres. EH5 —5G **7**
Crewe Gro. EH5 —5H **7**
Crewe Loan. EH5 —5G **7**
Crewe Path. EH5 —5G **7**
Crewe Pl. EH5 —5G **7**
Crewe Rd. Gdns. EH5 —5G **7**
Crewe Rd. N. EH5 —4G **7**
Crewe Rd. S. EH4 —6G **7**
Crewe Rd. W. EH5 —4G **7**
Crewe Ter. EH5 —5H **7**
Crichton St. EH8
—4H **15** (6F **3**)
Crighton Pl. EH7 —7E **8**
Croall Pl. EH7 —1J **15**
Crockett Gdns. EH26 —6A **34**
Croft-an-Righ. EH8
—2K **15** (2K **3**)
Croft St. EH22 —2F **33**
Cromwell Pl. EH6 —4E **8**
Crookston Rd. EH21 —4G **19**
(in three parts)
Cross Cotts. EH32 —3E **20**
Crosswood Av. EH14 —5D **28**
Crosswood Cres. EH14
—5D **28**
Crown Pl. EH6 —6E **8**
Crown St. EH6 —6E **8**
Cruachan Ct. EH26 —5D **34**
Crusader Dri. EH25 —1A **34**
Crystal Mt. EH22 —1F **33**
Cuddy La. EH10 —1E **24**
Cuguen Pl. EH19 —4A **32**
Cuiken Av. EH26 —5B **34**
Cuikenburn. EH26 —4B **34**
Cuiken Ter. EH26 —5A **34**
Cultins Rd. EH12 & EH11
—1D **22**
Cumberland St. EH3 —1G **15**

Cumberland St. N. E. La. EH3
—1G **15**
Cumberland St. N. W. La. EH3
—1G **15**
Cumberland St. S. E. La. EH3
—1G **15**
Cumberland St. S. W. La. EH3
—1G **15**
Cumin Pl. EH9 —6J **15**
Cumlodden Av. EH12 —3A **14**
Cumnor Cres. EH16 —3A **26**
Cunningham Pl. EH6 —6E **8**
Curriehill Castle Dri. EH14
—1F **29**
Currihill Rd. EH14 —7B **22**
Currievale Dri. EH14 —1G **29**
Currievale Pk. EH14 —1G **29**
Currievale Pk. Gro. EH14
—1G **29**
Cuthill. EH32 —3C **20**

Daiches Braes. EH15 —5J **17**
Daisy Ter. EH11 —7C **14**
Dalgety Av. EH7 —1B **16**
Dalgety Rd. EH7 —1B **16**
Dalgety St. EH7 —2B **16**
Dalhousie Av. EH19 —7K **31**
Dalhousie Av. W. EH19
—7K **31**
Dalhousie Dri. EH19 —7K **31**
Dalhousie Gdns. EH19
—7K **31**
Dalhousie Mains Cotts. EH22
—6D **32**
Dalhousie Pl. EH19 —7J **31**
Dalhousie Rd. EH22 —6D **32**
Dalhousie Rd. E. EH19
—7K **31**
Dalhousie Rd. W. EH19
—7K **31**
Dalhousie Ter. EH10 —2E **24**
Dalkeith Home Farm Cotts.
EH22 —7F **19**
Dalkeith Rd. EH8 —5K **15**
Dalkeith Rd. EH16 —6K **15**
Dalkeith St. EH15 —4J **17**
Dalmahoy Cres. EH14 —2D **28**
Dalmahoy Rd. EH28 —7B **10**
Dalmeny Rd. EH6 —5C **8**
Dalmeny St. EH6 —7E **8**
Dalrymple Cres. EH9 —7J **15**
Dalrymple Cres. EH21 —2C **18**
Dalrymple Loan. EH21 —2C **18**
Dalry Pl. EH11 —4E **14**
Dalry Rd. EH11 —5D **14**
Dalton Ct. EH22 —1K **35**
Dalum Ct. EH20 —5D **30**
Dalum Dri. EH20 —5D **30**
Dalum Gro. EH20 —5D **30**
Dalum Loan. EH20 —5D **30**
Dalziel Pl. EH7 —2B **16**
Damside. EH4 —3E **14**
Danderhall Cres. EH22
—5H **27**
Danube St. EH4 —2E **14**
D'arcy Rd. EH22 —7K **33**
Dark Wlk. EH22 —1G **35**
Darnaway St. EH3
—2F **15** (2A **2**)
Darnell Rd. EH5 —5K **7**
David Horn Ho. EH16 —1A **26**
David Scott Av. EH22 —6K **33**
Davidson Gdns. EH4 —7D **6**
Davidson Pk. EH4 —7H **7**
Davidson Rd. EH4 —7G **7**
Davie St. EH8 —4J **15** (6G **3**)
Dean Bank La. EH3 —1F **15**
Deanburn. EH26 —4B **34**
Deanery Clo. EH7 —2C **16**
Deanhaugh Path. EH4 —1F 15
(off Malta Ter.)
Deanhaugh St. EH4 —1F **15**
Dean Pk. EH22 —1F **35**
Deanpark Av. EH14 —4D **28**
Deanpark Bank. EH14 —4E **28**
Deanpark Brae. EH14 —4E **28**
Deanpark Ct. EH14 —5D **28**
Dean Pk. Ct. EH22 —1F **35**
Dean Pk. Cres. EH4 —2E **14**

Deanpark Cres. EH14 —4E **28**
Deanpark Gdns. EH14 —4E **28**
Deanpark Gro. EH14 —4E **28**
Dean Pk. M. EH4 —1E **14**
Deanpark Pl. EH22 —1F **35**
Deanpark Sq. EH14 —5E **28**
Dean Pk. St. EH4 —1E **14**
Dean Path. EH4 —2D **14**
Dean Path Bldgs. EH4 —3E 14
(off Dean Path)
Dean Pl. EH26 —5A **34**
Dean Rd. EH26 —5A **34**
Dean Ter. EH4 —1E **14**
Deantown Av. EH21 —7G **19**
Deantown Dri. EH21 —7G **19**
Deantown Path. EH21 —7G **19**
Dechmont Rd. EH12 —4C **12**
Delhaig. EH11 —7A **14**
Dell Rd. EH13 —5K **23**
Delta Av. EH21 —3J **19**
Delta Cres. EH21 —2J **19**
Delta Dri. EH21 —2J **19**
Delta Gdns. EH21 —3J **19**
Delta Pl. EH21 —4F **19**
Delta Rd. EH21 —3J **19**
Delta View. EH21 —2J **19**
Denham Grn. Av. EH5 —5A **8**
Denham Grn. Pl. EH5 —5A **8**
Denham Grn. Ter. EH5 —5A **8**
Denholm Rd. EH21 —4B **18**
Denholm Way. EH21 —4B **18**
De Quincey Path. EH18
—7H **31**
De Quincey Rd. EH18 —7H **31**
Dequincey Wlk. EH33 —7G **21**
Derby St. EH6 —4C **8**
Devon Pl. EH12 —4D **14**
Dewar Pl. EH3 —4E **14**
Dewar Pl. La. EH3 —4E **14**
Dick Pl. EH9 —7H **15**
Dickson Dri. EH19 —6A **32**
Dickson's Clo. EH1 —4G **3**
Dickson St. EH6 —7E **8**
Dick Ter. EH26 —5C **34**
Dinmont Dri. EH16 —3B **26**
Distillery La. EH11 —4D **14**
Dobbies Cotts. EH18 —1B **32**
Dobbies Rd. EH18 & EH19
—6K **31**
Dochart Dri. EH4 —2E **12**
Dock Pl. EH6 —4E **8**
Dock St. EH6 —4E **8**
Dolphin Av. EH14 —1H **29**
Dolphin Gdns. E. EH14
—1H **29**
Dolphin Gdns. W. EH14
—1G **29**
Dolphin Rd. EH14 —2G **29**
Doo'cot Pl. EH32 —4D **20**
Dorset Pl. EH11 —6E **14**
Double Dykes. EH4 —4F **19**
Double Hedges Pk. EH16
—3A **26**
Double Hedges Rd. EH16
—3A **26**
Dougall Ct. EH22 —1J **35**
Dougall Pl. EH22 —1J **35**
Dougall Rd. EH22 —1J **35**
Douglas Cres. EH12 —3D **14**
Douglas Cres. EH19 —6A **32**
Douglas Gdns. EH4 —3D **14**
Douglas Gdns. M. EH4
—3D **14**
Douglas Ter. EH11 —4E **14**
Doune Ter. EH3 —2F **15** (1A **2**)
Dovecot Brae. EH33 —5G **21**
Dovecot Gro. EH14 —3J **23**
Dovecot Loan. EH14 —3J **23**
Dovecot Pk. EH14 —4J **23**
Dovecot Rd. EH12 —5E **13**
Dow Craig. EH32 —3C **20**
Dowie's Mill Cotts. EH4 —6H **5**
Dowie's Mill La. EH4 —6G **5**
Downfield Pl. EH11 —5D **14**
Downie Gro. EH12 —5H **13**
Downie Pl. EH21 —2E **18**
Downie Ter. EH12 —5H **13**
Dreghorn Av. EH13 —7C **24**

Dreghorn Cotts. EH13 —7B **24**
Dreghorn Dri. EH13 —7C **24**
Dreghorn Gdns. EH13 —7C **24**
Dreghorn Gro. EH13 —7D **24**
Dreghorn Link. EH13 —7C **24**
Dreghorn Loan. EH13
　　　　　—6K **23**
Dreghorn Pk. EH13 —6B **24**
Dreghorn Pl. EH13 —7C **24**
Drum Av. EH17 —6E **26**
Drum Brae Av. EH12 —3E **12**
Drum Brae Cres. EH4 —2E **12**
Drum Brae Dri. EH4 —2E **12**
Drum Brae Gdns. EH12
　　　　　—3E **12**
Drum Brae Gro. EH4 —2E **12**
Drum Brae Junction. EH4
　　　　　—1D **12**
Drum Brae Neuk. EH12
　　　　　—3E **12**
Drum Brae N. EH4 —1D **12**
Drum Brae Pk. EH12 —3E **12**
Drum Brae Pk. App. EH12
　　　　　—3E **12**
Drum Brae Pl. EH12 —3E **12**
Drum Brae S. EH12 —2E **12**
Drum Brae Ter. EH4 —2E **12**
Drum Brae Wlk. EH4 —2D **12**
(in three parts)
Drum Cotts. EH17 —7F **27**
Drum Cres. EH17 —6F **27**
Drumdryan St. EH3
　　　　　—5F **15** (7B **2**)
Drummohr Av. EH21 —3J **19**
Drummohr Gdns. EH21
　　　　　—3K **19**
Drummond Pl. EH3 —1G **15**
Drummond St. EH8
　　　　　—4J **15** (5G **3**)
Drummore Dri. EH32 —4C **20**
Drum Pl. EH17 —6F **27**
Drumsheugh Gdns. EH3
　　　　　—3E **14**
Drumsheugh Pl. EH3 —3E **14**
(off Drumsheugh Gdns.)
Drum St. EH17　6E **26**
Drum Ter. EH7 —1A **16**
Dryden Av. EH22 —5H **27**
Dryden Av. EH20 —6D **30**
Dryden Cres. EH20 —6D **30**
Dryden Gdns. EH7 —7D **8**
Dryden Gro. EH25 —1B **34**
Dryden Pl. EH9 —6K **15**
Dryden St. EH7 —7D **8**
Dryden Ter. EH7 —7D **8**
Dryden Ter. EH20 —6D **30**
Dryden View. EH20 —6D **30**
Drylaw Av. EH4 —1K **13**
Drylaw Cres. EH4 —1K **13**
Drylaw Gdns. EH4 —7E **6**
Drylaw Grn. EH4 —1K **13**
Drylaw Gro. EH4 —1K **13**
Drylaw Ho. Gdns. EH4 —7E **6**
Drylaw Ho. Paddock. EH4
　　　　　—7E **6**
Duart Cres. EH4 —2E **12**
Dublin Meuse. EH3
　　　　　—2G **15** (1D **2**)
Dublin St. EH17　6E **26**
Dublin St. EH3 & EH1 —1H **15**
Dublin St. La. N. EH3 —1H **15**
Dublin St. La. S. EH1
　　　　　—2H **15** (1E **2**)
Duddingston Av. EH15
　　　　　—5E **16**
Duddingston Cres. EH15
　　　　　—5G **17**
Duddingston Gdns. N. EH15
　　　　　—4F **17**
Duddingston Gdns. S. EH15
　　　　　—5F **17**
Duddingston Gro. E. EH15
　　　　　—4F **17**
Duddingston Gro. W. EH15
　　　　　—5F **17**
Duddingston Loan. EH15
　　　　　—4E **16**
Duddingston Mains Cotts.
　　　EH15 —5H **17**
Duddingston Mills Cotts. EH8
　　　　　—4E **16**

Duddingston Pk. EH15
　　　　　—4G **17**
Duddingston Pk. S. EH15
　　　　　—5G **17**
Duddingston Rise. EH15
　　　　　—5F **17**
Duddingston Rd. EH15
　　　　　—4E **16**
Duddingston Rd. W. EH15 &
　　　EH16 —5D **16**
Duddingston Row. EH15
　　　　　—5F **17**
Duddingston Sq. E. EH15
　　　　　—4F **17**
Duddingston Sq. W. EH15
　　　　　—4F **17**
Duddingston View. EH15
　　　　　—5F **17**
Duddingston Yards. EH15
　　　　　—6G **17**
Dudgeon Pl. EH29 —1B **10**
Dudley Av. EH6 —4C **8**
Dudley Av. S. EH6 —5D **8**
Dudley Bank. EH6 —4C **8**
Dudley Cres. EH6 —4C **8**
Dudley Gdns. EH6 —4C **8**
Dudley Gro. EH6 —4C **8**
Dudley Ter. EH6 —4C **8**
Duff St. EH11 —5D **14**
Duff St. La. EH11 —5D **14**
Duke Pl. EH6 —6F **9**
Duke St. EH6 —6F **9**
Duke St. EH22 —2F **33**
Duke St. EH24 —7F **35**
Duke's Wlk. EH8 —2B **16**
Dumbiedykes Rd. EH8
　　　　　—4K **15** (5J **3**)
Dumbryden Dri. EH14 —3G **23**
Dumbryden Gdns. EH14
　　　　　—2G **23**
Dumbryden Gro. EH14
　　　　　—3G **23**
Dumbryden Rd. EH14 —3H **23**
Dun-Ard Garden. EH9 —1H **25**
Dunbar's Clo. EH8 —3H **3**
Dunbar St. EH3 —5F **15** (6B **2**)
Duncan Gdns. EH33 —5G **21**
Duncan Pl. EH6 —6F **9**
Duncan Gait. EH14 —2J **23**
Duncan St. EH9 —7J **15**
Dundas Av. EH30 —6C **4**
Dundas Cres. EH22 —4D **32**
Dundas Gro. EH22 —3D **32**
Dundas Pk. EH19 —6B **32**
Dundas Pl. EH29 —1B **10**
Dundas Rd. EH22 —3D **32**
Dundas St. EH3 —1G **15**
Dundas St. EH19 —6B **32**
Dundee St. EH11 —6D **14**
Dundee Ter. EH11 —6D **14**
Dundonald St. EH3 —1G **15**
Dundrennan Cotts. EH16
　　　　　—2C **26**
Dunedin St. EH7 —7C **8**
Dunlop's Ct. EH1 —5D **2**
Dunlop Ter. EH26 —6D **34**
Dunollie Ct. EH4 —6H **5**
Dunrobin Pl. EH3 —7A **8**
Dunsmuir Ct. EH12 —5E **12**
Dunsyre Ho. EH11 —3E **22**
Dunvegan Ct. EH4 —6J **5**
Durar Dri. EH4 —3E **12**
Durham Av. EH15 —4F **17**
Durham Bank. EH19 —7B **32**
Durham Dri. EH15 —5G **17**
Durham Gdns. N. EH15
　　　　　—4F **17**
Durham Gdns. S. EH15
　　　　　—5G **17**
Durham Gro. EH15 —4G **17**
Durham Gro. EH19 —7B **32**
Durham Pl. EH19 —7A **32**
Durham Pl. E. EH15 —4G **17**
Durham Pl. La. EH15 —4F **17**
Durham Pl. W. EH15 —4F **17**
Durham Rd. EH15 —4G **17**
Durham Rd. S. EH15 —5G **17**
Durham Sq. EH15 —4F **17**
Durham Ter. EH15 —4F **17**
Durward Gro. EH16 —2B **26**

E. Montgomery Pl. EH7
　　　　　—1K **15**
E. Newington Pl. EH9 —6K **15**
E. Norton Pl. EH7 —1K **3**
E. Parkside. EH16 —5K **15**
E. Preston St. EH8 —6J **15**
E. Preston St. La. EH8 —6K **15**
E. Queensway. EH26 —4C **34**
E. Restalrig Ter. EH6 —6G **9**
E. Savile Rd. EH16 —1K **25**
E. Sciennes St. EH9 —6J **15**
E. Seaside. EH32 —2D **20**
E. Silvermills La. EH3 —1F **15**
(in two parts)
E. Straiton Cotts. EH20
(off Straiton Rd.) —3D **30**
E. Suffolk Rd. EH16 —1A **26**
E. Telferton. EH7 —2F **17**
East Ter. EH30 —5C **4**
E. Trinity Rd. EH5 —5A **8**
East Way, The. EH8 —3E **16**
Echline. EH30 —6A **4**
Echline Av. EH30 —6A **4**
Echline Gdns. EH30 —5A **4**
Echline Grn. EH30 —5A **4**
Echline Pk. EH30 —6A **4**
Echline Pl. EH30 —6A **4**
Echline Rigg. EH30 —5A **4**
Echline Ter. EH30 —6A **4**
Echline View. EH30 —6A **4**
Edenhall Bank. EH21 —3G **19**
Edenhall Cres. EH21 —3G **19**
Edenhall Rd. EH21 —3G **19**
Eden La. EH10 —1F **25**
Edgefield Farm Cotts. EH20
　　　　　—4F **31**
Edgefield Pl. EH20 —5F **31**
Edgefield Rd. EH20 —5F **31**
Edgefield Rd. Ind. Est. EH20
　　　　　—4E **30**
Edina Pl. EH7 —1A **16**
Edina St. EH7 —1K **15**
Edinburgh Airport. FH12
　　　　　—3F **11**
Edinburgh Pk. EH12 —6B **12**
Edinburgh Rd. EH21 —1B **18**
Edinburgh Rd. EH22 —2F **33**
Edinburgh Rd. EH26 —5C **34**
Edinburgh Rd. EH30 —5C **4**
Edinburgh Rd. EH32 —1E **20**
Edinburgh Rd. EH33 —6F **21**
Edinburgh Waverley Sta. EH1
　　　　　—3H **15** (3F **3**)
Edmonstone Av. EH22
　　　　　—4H **27**
Edmonstone Dri. EH22
　　　　　—4H **27**
Edmonstone Rd. EH22
　　　　　—4G **27**
Edmonstone Ter. EH22
　　　　　—4H **27**
Eglinton Cres. EH12 —4D **14**
Eglinton St. EH12 —4C **14**
Egypt M. EH10 —2G **25**
Eighth St. EH22 —1G **35**
Eildon St. EH3 —7B **8**
Eildon Ter. EH3 —6A **8**
Elbe St. EH6 —5F **9**
Elcho Pl. EH32 —1A **20**
Elcho Ter. EH15 —3J **17**
Elder St. EH1 —2H **15** (1F **3**)
Elder St. EH33 —5G **21**
Elder St. E. EH1
　　　　　—2H **15** (1F **3**)
Eldindean Pl. EH19 —5A **32**
Eldindean Rd. EH19 —5A **32**
Eldindean Ter. EH19 —5A **32**
Eldin Ind. Est. EH20 —3F **31**
Electra Pl. EH15 —2G **17**
Elginhaugh Cotts. EH22
　　　　　—2C **32**
Elgin Pl. EH12 —4D **14**
Elgin St. EH7 —1K **15**
Elgin St. N. EH7 —1K **15**
Elgin Ter. EH7 —1K **15**
Elizafield. EH6 —6D **8**
Ellangowan Ter. EH16 —3C **26**
Ellen's Glen Rd. EH17 —6C **26**
Ellersly Rd. EH12 —4K **13**
Elliot Gdns. EH14 —4A **24**

Elliot Pk. EH14 —4A **24**
Elliot Pl. EH14 —4A **24**
Elliot Rd. EH14 —4A **24**
Elliot St. EH7 —1K **15**
Elliott's Clo. EH22 —2F **33**
(off High St. Dalkeith)
Elmfield Ct. EH22 —2F **33**
Elmfield Pk. EH22 —2F **33**
Elmfield Rd. EH22 —2F **33**
Elm Pl. EH6 —6G **9**
Elm Pl. EH22 —7J **33**
Elm Row. EH7 —1J **15**
(in two parts)
Elm Row. EH18 —4K **31**
Elmwood Ter. EH6 —7G **9**
Elphinstone Ct. EH33 —6G **21**
Elphinstone Rd. EH33 —7F **21**
Elphinstone Wlk. EH33
　　　　　—7G **21**
Eltringham Gdns. EH14
　　　　　—7A **14**
Eltringham Gro. EH14 —7A **14**
Eltringham Ter. EH14 —7A **14**
Elvanbank Cotts. EH11
　　　　　—5B **14**
Emily Ct. EH23 —5H **35**
Emily Pl. EH23 —5J **35**
Engine Rd. EH20 —5F **31**
Engine Rd. EH23 —5G **35**
Eskbank Ind. Est. EH22
　　　　　—5D **32**
Eskbank Rd. EH19 & EH22
　　　　　—5B **32**
Eskbank Rd. EH22 —3E **32**
Eskbank Rd. Roundabout.
　　　　　FH22 —5C **32**
Eskbank Ter. EH22 —3E **32**
Eskbank Toll. EH22 —3D **32**
Eskdaill Ct. EH22 —2F **33**
(off Eskdaill St.)
Eskdaill St. EH22 —2F **33**
Eskdale Ct. EH19 —6K **31**
Eskdale Dri. EH19 —6K **31**
Eskdale M. EH21 —2E **18**
Eskdale Ter. EH19 —6K **31**
Esk Glades. EH22 —6A **32**
Eskgrove Dri. EH25 —7B **30**
Eskhill. EH26 —6C **34**
Eskmill Ind. Est. EH26 —6D **34**
Eskmill Rd. EH26 —6D **34**
Eskmill Vs. EH21 —3D **10**
Esk Pl. EH22 —2E **32**
Eskside Ct. EH22 —1E **32**
Eskside E. EH21 —2E **18**
Eskside W. EH21 —3D **18**
Eskvale Cres. EH26 —6D **34**
Eskvale Dri. EH26 —5D **34**
Eskview Av. EH21 —3D **18**
Eskview Cres. EH21 —3D **18**
Eskview Gro. EH21 —3D **18**
Eskview Gro. EH22 —2E **32**
Eskview Rd. EH21 —3D **18**
Eskview Rd. EH22 —7J **33**
Eskview Ter. EH21 —3D **18**
Eskview Vs. EH22 —2D **32**
Esplanade. EH1 —3G **15**
Esplanade Ter. EH15 —3K **17**
Essendean Pl. EH4 —2F **13**
Essendean Ter. EH4 —2F **13**
Essex Brae. EH4 —6H **5**
Essex Pk. EH4 —6H **5**
Essex Rd. EH4 —6H **5**
Esslemont Rd. EH16 —2K **25**
Ethel Ter. EH10 —2E **24**
Eton Ter. EH4 —2E **14**
Ettrickdale Pl. EH3 —1F **15**
Ettrick Gro. EH10 —6E **14**
Ettrick Rd. EH10 —7D **14**
Evans Gdns. EH19 —5C **32**
Eva Pl. EH9 —2J **25**
Ewerland. EH4 —6H **5**
Ewing St. EH26 —4C **34**
Eyre Cres. EH3 —1G **15**
Eyre Pl. EH3 —1G **15**
Eyre Ter. EH3 —1G **15**

Dyke's Rd. EH26 —4B **34**

Earl Grey St. EH3
　　　　　—4F **15** (6B **2**)
Earl Haig Gdns. EH5 —5A **8**
Earlston Pl. EH7 —2A **16**
E. Adam St. EH8
　　　　　—4J **15** (5G **3**)
E. Barnton Av. EH4 —7B **6**
E. Barnton Av. EH4 —7B **6**
E. Barnton Gdns. EH4 —7B **6**
E. Brighton Cres. EH15
　　　　　—3G **17**
E. Broughton Pl. EH1 —1H **15**
E. Caiystane Pl. EH10 —6E **24**
E. Caiystane Rd. EH10 —6E **24**
E. Castle Rd. EH10 —6E **14**
E. Champanyie. EH9 —1J **25**
E. Clapperfield. EH16 —3A **26**
E. Claremont St. EH7 —1H **15**
E. Comiston. EH10 —6E **24**
East Ct. EH4 —2A **14**
East Ct. EH16 —1F **27**
East Croft. EH28 —7C **10**
E. Cromwell St. EH6 —4E **8**
E. Crosscauseway. EH8
　　　　　—5J **15** (7G **3**)
Easter Belmont Rd. EH12
　　　　　—4K **13**
Easter Currie Ct. EH14 —1J **29**
Easter Currie Cres. EH14
　　　　　—7C **22**
Easter Currie Pl. EH14 —7C **22**
Easter Currie Ter. EH14
　　　　　—1J **29**
Easter Drylaw Av. EH4 —7F **7**
Easter Drylaw Bank. EH4
　　　　　—6F **7**
Easter Drylaw Dri. EH4 —7F **7**
Easter Drylaw Gdns. EH4
　　　　　—7F **7**
Easter Drylaw Gro. EH4 —7F **7**
Easter Drylaw Loan. EH4
　　　　　—7F **7**
Easter Drylaw Pl. EH4 —6F **7**
Easter Drylaw View. EH4
　　　　　—6G **7**
Easter Drylaw Way. EH4
　　　　　—7F **7**
Easter Halles Ga. EH13 & EH14
　　　　　—4J **23**
Easter Haugh. EH13 —5C **24**
Eastern Ind. Est. EH15 —7J **17**
Easter Pk. Dri. EH4 —6B **6**
Easter Pk. Ho. EH4 —6B **6**
Easter Rd. EH7 & EH6
　　　　　—2K **15** (1K **3**)
Easter Steil. EH10 —3D **24**
Easter Warriston. EH7 —6B **8**
E. Farm of Gilmerton. EH17
　　　　　—6E **26**
E. Fettes Av. EH4 —6J **7**
Eastfield. EH15 —1B **18**
Eastfield. EH26 —5C **34**
Eastfield Dri. EH26 —5C **34**
Eastfield Farm Rd. EH26
　　　　　—4C **34**
Eastfield Gdns. EH15 —1A **18**
Eastfield Ind. Est. EH26
　　　　　—5C **34**
Eastfield Pk. Rd. EH26 —5C **34**
Eastfield Pl. EH15 —1B **18**
Eastfield Rd. EH28 —4G **11**
E. Hannahfield. EH14 —3C **28**
E. Hermitage Pl. EH6 —6F **9**
Easthouses Ct. EH22 —5H **33**
Easthouses Ind. Est. EH22
　　　　　—5J **33**
Easthouses Pl. EH22 —4J **33**
Easthouses Rd. EH22 —3H **33**
Easthouses Way. EH22
　　　　　—4H **33**
E. Lillypot. EH5 —5A **8**
E. Loan. EH32 —2D **20**
E. London St. EH7 —1H **15**
E. Lorimer Pl. EH32 —1A **20**
E. Market St. EH1
　　　　　—3H **15** (3F **3**)
E. Mayfield. EH9 —7K **15**

Fairhaven Vs. EH22 —4D **32**
Fairmile Av. EH10 —6F **25**
Fairmilehead. EH10 —7F **25**
Fairview Rd. EH28 —4F **11**
Fairways, The. EH21 —4D **18**
Fala Ct. EH16 —6B **26**
Falcon Av. EH10 —1F **25**
Falcon Ct. EH10 —1F **25**
Falcon Gdns. EH10 —1F **25**
Falcon Rd. EH10 —1F **25**
Falcon Rd. W. EH10 —1F **25**
Falkland Gdns. EH12 —2G **13**
Farm Av. EH18 —7J **31**
Farquhar Ter. EH30 —5A **4**
Farrer Gro. EH7 —2F **17**
Farrer Ter. EH7 —2E **16**
Fa'side Av. EH33 —7H **21**
Fa'side Av. Ct. EH21 —4K **19**
Fa'side Av. N. EH21 —4K **19**
Fa'side Av. S. EH21 —4K **19**
Fa'side Cres. EH21 —4K **19**
Fa'side Cres. EH33 —7H **21**
Fa'side Dri. EH21 —4K **19**
Fa'side Gdns. EH21 —4K **19**
Fa'side Rd. EH33 —7H **21**
Fa'side Ter. EH21 —4K **19**
Fauldburn. EH12 —2D **12**
Fauldburn Pk. EH12 —2D **12**
Featherhall Av. EH12 —5F **13**
Featherhall Cres. N. EH12 —5E **12**
Featherhall Cres. S. EH12 —5E **12**
Featherhall Gro. EH12 —5F **13**
Featherhall Pl. EH12 —5F **13**
Featherhall Rd. EH12 —5F **13**
Featherhall Ter. EH12 —5F **13**
Felton Grn. EH21 —3F **19**
Ferguson Ct. EH21 —5E **18**
Ferguson Dri. EH21 —5D **18**
Ferguson Gdns. EH21 —5E **18**
Ferguson Grn. EH21 —5D **18**
Ferguson View. EH21 —5D **18**
Ferguson Way. EH22 —2G **35**
Ferniehill Av. EH17 —6E **26**
Ferniehill Dri. EH17 —6E **26**
Ferniehill Gdns. EH17 —5F **27**
Ferniehill Gro. EH17 —5F **27**
Ferniehill Pl. EH17 —6E **26**
Ferniehill Rd. EH17 —6E **26**
Ferniehill Sq. EH17 —6E **26**
Ferniehill St. EH17 —5E **26**
Ferniehill Ter. EH17 —6E **26**
Ferniehill Way. EH17 —5F **27**
Fernielaw Av. EH13 —7J **23**
Fernieside Av. EH17 —5E **26**
Fernieside Cres. EH17 —5E **26**
Fernieside Dri. EH17 —4E **26**
Fernieside Gdns. EH17 —5E **26**
Fernieside Gro. EH17 —5F **27**
Ferryburn. EH30 —6C 4
(off Rosebery Av.)
Ferryburn Grn. EH30 —6C **4**
Ferryfield. EH5 —6J **7**
Ferrymuir La. EH30 —6B **4**
Ferry Rd. EH4 —7D **6**
Ferry Rd. EH5 & EH6 —6H **7**
Ferry Rd. Av. EH4 —6F **7**
Ferry Rd. Dri. EH4 —5G **7**
Ferry Rd. Gdns. EH4 —6F **7**
Ferry Rd. Gro. EH4 —6F **7**
Ferry Rd. Pl. EH4 —6F **7**
Festival Sq. EH3 —4F **15** (5B **2**)
Fetteresk Cotts. EH26 —7B **34**
Fettes Av. EH4 —1D **14**
Fettes Rise. EH4 —6J **7**
Fettes Row. EH3 —1G **15**
Fidra Ct. EH4 —5D **6**
Fifth St. EH22 —1F **35**
Figgate Bank. EH15 —2H **17**
Figgate La. EH15 —2H **17**
Figgate St. EH15 —2G **17**
Fillyside Av. EH7 —1E **16**
Fillyside Rd. EH7 —7K **9**
Fillyside Ter. EH7 —7K **9**
Findhorn Pl. EH9 —6J **15**
Findlay Av. EH7 —7H **9**
Findlay Cotts. EH7 —7H **9**
Findlay Gdns. EH7 —7H **9**
Findlay Gro. EH7 —7H **9**
Findlay Medway. EH7 —7H **9**
Fingal Pl. EH9 —6H **15**
Fingzies Pl. EH6 —6G **9**
Finlaggan Ct. EH12 —3C **12**
Finlay Pl. EH22 —7K **33**
Firrhill Cres. EH13 —4C **24**
Firrhill Dri. EH13 —5C **24**
Firrhill Loan. EH13 —5C **24**
First Gait. EH14 —4A **22**
First St. EH22 —2G **35**
Fir View. EH20 —6C 30
(off Nivensknowe Caravan Pk.)
Fishergate Rd. EH32 —1C **20**
Fisherrow Ind. Est. EH21 —2C **18**
Fishers Rd. EH32 —1B **20**
Fishers Wynd. EH21 —2D **18**
Fishmarket Sq. EH6 —3C **8**
Fishwives Causeway. EH8 & (in three parts) EH15 —2E **16**
Fleets Gro. EH33 —7H **21**
Fleets Rd. EH33 —7G **21**
Fleets View. EH33 —7H **21**
Fleshmarket Clo. EH1 —4F **3**
Fletcher Gro. EH26 —3C **34**
Forbes Rd. EH10 —7F **15**
Forbes St. EH8 —5J **15** (7H **3**)
Ford's Rd. EH11 —7K **13**
Forester's View. EH33 —6H **21**
Forres St. EH3 —2F **15** (2A **2**)
Forrester Pk. Av. EH12 —7F **13**
Forrester Pk. Dri. EH12 —7F **13**
Forrester Pk. Gdns. EH12 —7F **13**
Forrester Pk. Grn. EH12 —7G **13**
Forrester Pk. Gro. EH12 —7F **13**
Forrester Pk. Loan. EH12 —7F **13**
Forrester Rd. EH12 —4F **13**
Forrest Hill. EH1 —4H **15** (6E **2**)
Forrest Rd. EH1 —4H **15** (6E **2**)
Forteviot Ho. EH17 —4D **26**
Forth Ct. EH32 —1C **20**
Forth Gdns. EH32 —1C **20**
Forth Gro. EH32 —1C **20**
Fort Ho. EH6 —4D **8**
Forth Pl. EH30 —5A **4**
Forth St. EH1 —2H **15** (1F **3**)
Forth Ter. EH30 —6D **4**
Forth View. EH15 —7J **17**
Forth View Av. EH14 —1H **29**
Forthview Av. EH21 —3J **19**
Forth View Cres. EH14 —7B **22**
Forthview Cres. EH21 —3J **19**
Forth View Cres. EH22 —4H **27**
Forthview Dri. EH21 —4J **19**
Forthview Rd. EH4 —1A **14**
Forth View Rd. EH14 —1H **29**
Forthview Ter. EH4 —1K **13**
Forthview Ter. EH21 —3K **19**
Forth Wynd. EH32 —1C **20**
Foulis Cres. EH14 —6F **23**
Foundry La. EH20 —5F **31** (in two parts)
Fountainbridge. EH3 —5E **14**
Fountain Clo. EH1 —4G **3**
Fountainhall Rd. EH9 —1J **25**
Fountain Pl. EH20 —5F **31**
Fourth Gait. EH14 —5A **22**
Fourth St. EH22 —1F **35**
Fowler Cres. EH20 —5G **31**
Fowler's Ct. EH32 —2E **20**
Fowler Sq. EH20 —5G **31**
Fowler St. EH33 —5G **21**
Fowler Ter. EH11 —6D **14**
Fox Covert Av. EH12 —2G **13**
Fox Covert Gro. EH12 —2G **13**
Fox Spring Cres. EH10 —5E **24**
Fox Spring Rise. EH10 —5E **24**
Fox St. EH6 —5G **9**
Fraser Av. EH5 —5K **7**
Fraser Cres. EH5 —5K **7**
Fraser Gdns. EH5 —5K **7**
Fraser Gro. EH5 —5K **7**
Frederick St. EH2 —2G **15** (2C **2**)
Freelands Cotts. EH28 —7F **11**
Freelands Rd. EH28 —7E **10**
Freer St. EH3 —5F **15** (7A **2**)
Friarton Gdns. EH26 —7A **34**
Frogston Av. EH10 —7F **25**
Frogston Gdns. EH10 —7F **25**
Frogston Gro. EH10 —7G **25**
Frogston Rd. E. EH16 & EH17 —1B **30**
Frogston Rd. W. EH10 & EH16 —7F **25**
Frogston Ter. EH10 —7G **25**
Gabriel's Rd. EH2 —2F **3**
Gabriel's Rd. EH3 —1F **15**
Galachlawshot. EH10 —6G **25**
Galachlawside. EH10 —7G **25**
Galadale. EH22 —7F **33**
Galadale Cres. EH22 —7F **33**
Galadale Dri. EH22 —7F **33**
Gallolee, The. EH13 —6B **24**
Galloway's Entry. EH8 —3K **15** (3J **3**)
Galt Av. EH21 —2H **19**
Galt Cres. EH21 —3J **19**
Galt Dri. EH21 —3J **19**
Galt Rd. EH21 —3J **19**
Galt Ter. EH21 —3J **19**
Gamekeeper's Loan. EH4 —5J **5**
Gamekeeper's Pk. EH4 —5J **5**
Gamekeeper's Rd. EH4 —6J **5**
Gardener's Clo. EH32 —1A **20**
Gardener's Cres. EH3 —6A **2**
Gardener's Pl. EH33 —5G **21**
Gardener's Wlk. EH26 —5A **34**
Garden Ter. EH4 —6A **6**
Gardiner Cres. EH32 —3F **21**
Gardiner Gro. EH4 —1K **13**
Gardiner Pl. EH22 —7F **33**
Gardiner Rd. EH4 —1K **13**
Gardiner Rd. EH32 —3E **20**
Gardiner Ter. EH4 —2K **13**
Gardiner Ter. EH32 —4E **20**
Gardner's Cres. EH3 —4F **15**
Gardner St. EH7 —2A 16
(off Lwr. London Rd.)
Garscube Ter. EH12 —3B **14**
Garvald Ct. EH16 —6B **26**
Gateside Rd. EH29 —2A **10**
Gayfield Clo. EH1 —1J **15**
Gayfield Pl. EH7 —1J **15**
Gayfield Pl. La. EH1 —1J **15**
Gayfield Sq. EH1 —1J **15**
Gayfield St. EH1 —1J **15**
Gaynor Av. EH20 —5D **30**
Gedden's Entry. EH1 —4F **3**
George Av. EH20 —5E **30**
George Cres. EH20 —5F **31**
George Dri. EH20 —5E **30**
George IV Bri. EH1 —3H **15** (4E **2**)
George Sq. EH8 —5H **15** (7F **3**)
George Sq. La. EH8 —5H **15** (7E **2**)
George St. EH2 —3F **15** (3B **2**)
George Ter. EH20 —5E **30**
George Wlk. EH33 —7G **21**
George Way. EH33 —6G **21**
Gibb's Entry. EH8 —4J **15**
Gibraltar Ct. EH22 —2G **33**
Gibraltar Gdns. EH22 —2F **33**
Gibraltar Rd. EH22 —2F **33**
Gibraltar Ter. EH22 —2G **33**
Gibson Dri. EH22 —2H **33**
Gibson St. EH7 —6D **8**
Gibson Ter. EH11 —5E **14**
Gifford Pk. EH8 —5J **15**
Gilberstoun. EH15 —5J **17**
Gilberstoun Brig. EH15 —6J **17**
Gilberstoun Loan. EH15 —6K **17**
Gilberstoun Pl. EH15 —6J **17**
Gilberstoun Wynd. EH15 —6K **17**
Giles St. EH6 —5E **8**
Gillespie Cres. EH10 —5F **15**
Gillespie Pl. EH10 —5F **15**
Gillespie Rd. EH13 —6H **23**
Gillespie St. EH3 —5F **15**
Gillsland Gro. EH10 —7D **14**
Gillsland Pk. EH10 —7D **14**
Gillsland Rd. EH10 —7D **14**
Gilmerton Dykes Av. EH17 —7C **26**
Gilmerton Dykes Cres. EH17 —6C **26**
Gilmerton Dykes Dri. EH17 —6D **26**
Gilmerton Dykes Gdns. EH17 —6C **26**
Gilmerton Dykes Gro. EH17 —6C **26**
Gilmerton Dykes Loan. EH17 —7D **26**
Gilmerton Dykes Pl. EH17 —6C **26**
Gilmerton Dykes Rd. EH17 —1G **31**
Gilmerton Dykes St. EH17 —7C **26**
Gilmerton Dykes Ter. EH17 —7D **26**
Gilmerton Dykes View. EH17 —7D **26**
Gilmerton Junction. EH18 —1K **31**
Gilmerton Pl. EH17 —7D **26**
Gilmerton Rd. EH16 & EH17 —2A **26**
Gilmerton Rd. EH17, EH16 & EH22 —7F **27**
Gilmerton Sta. Rd. EH17 —2H **31**
Gilmore Pk. EH3 —5E **14**
Gilmore Pl. EH3 —6E **14**
Gilmore Pl. La. EH3 —5F **15**
Gilmour Rd. EH16 —1K **25**
Gilmour's Clo. EH1 —5D **2**
Gilmour's Entry. EH8 —4J **15** (6H **3**)
Gilmour St. EH8 —4J **15** (6H **3**)
Girdle Wlk. EH32 —3C **20**
Gladstone Pl. EH6 —6G **9**
Gladstone Ter. EH9 —6J **15**
Glasgow Rd. EH28 & EH12 —5B **10**
Glaskhill Ter. EH26 —5B **34**
Glebe Gdns. EH12 —5G **13**
Glebe Gdns. EH32 —3D **20**
Glebe Gro. EH12 —5F **13**
Glebe Pl. EH18 —4J **31**
Glebe Rd. EH12 —5F **13**
Glebe St. EH22 —2F **33**
Glebe Ter. EH12 —5F **13**
Glebe, The. EH4 —4J **5**
Glebe, The. EH29 —2A **10**
Glebe, The. EH30 —7E **4**
Glenallan Dri. EH16 —2B **26**
Glenallan Loan. EH16 —2B **26**
Glenalmond Ct. EH11 —2F 23
(off Sighthill Bank)
Glenbrook. EH14 —5A **28**
Glenbrook Rd. EH14 —5A **28**
Glencairn Cres. EH12 —4D **14**
Glencorse Ho. EH4 —7J **7**
Glencross Gdns. EH26 —7A **34**
Glendevon Av. EH12 —5K **13**
Glendevon Gdns. EH12 —5K **13**
Glendevon Gro. EH12 —5K **13**
Glendevon Pk. EH12 —5K **13**
Glendevon Pl. EH12 —3E **6**
Glendevon Rd. EH12 —6K **13**
Glendevon Ter. EH12 —5K **13**
Glendinning Cres. EH16 —4A **26**
Glenesk Cres. EH22 —3E **32**
Glenfinlas St. EH3 —3F **15** (3A **2**)
Glengyle Ter. EH3 —5F **15**
Glenisla Gdns. EH9 —1H **25**
Glenisla Gdns. La. EH9 —1H **25**
Glenlea Cotts. EH11 —7A **14**
Glenlee Av. EH8 —3C **16**
Glenlee Gdns. EH8 —3C **16**
Glenlockhart Bank. EH14 —3B **24**
Glenlockhart Rd. EH14 & EH10 —3B **24**
Glenlockhart Valley. EH14 —2B **24**
Glennie Gdns. EH33 —6H **21**
Glenogle Ho. EH3 —1F **15**
Glenogle Pl. EH3 —1F **15**
Glenogle Rd. EH3 —1F **15**
Glenogle Ter. EH3 —7A **8**
Glenorchy Pl. EH1 —2J **15** (1G **3**)
Glenorchy Ter. EH9 —7K **15**
Glenpark. EH14 —4B **28**
Glen Pl. EH26 —5B **34**
Glen St. EH3 —5G **15** (6C **2**)
Glenure Loan. EH4 —2F **13**
Glenvarloch Cres. EH16 —3B **26**
Glenview. EH26 —5B **34**
Glen View Ct. EH23 —6H **35**
Glen View Cres. EH23 —6H **35**
Glenview Pl. EH23 —7H **35**
Glen View Rd. EH23 —5H **35**
Gloucester La. EH3 —2F **15** (1A **2**)
Gloucester Pl. EH3 —2F **15** (1A **2**)
Gloucester Sq. EH3 —2F **15** (1A **2**)
Gloucester St. EH3 —2F **15** (1A **2**)
Glover St. EH6 —6F **9**
Goff Av. EH7 —1F **17**
Gogap Roundabout. EH12 —5A **12**
Gogarbank. EH12 —2A **22**
Gogarbank Cotts. EH12 —1A **22**
Gogarloch Haugh. EH12 —6D **12**
Gogarloch Muir. EH12 —6D **12**
Gogarloch Rd. EH12 —6C **12**
Gogarloch Syke. EH12 —6C **12**
Gogar Mains Farm Rd. EH12 —4J **11**
Gogar Sta. Rd. EH12 —6K **11** (in two parts)
Goldenacre Ter. EH3 —6A **8**
Goldie Ter. EH20 —6D **30**
Golf Course Rd. EH19 —5A **32**
Golf Dri. EH32 —1C **20**
Goose Grn. Av. EH21 —1F **19**
Goose Grn. Bri. EH21 —1E **18**
Goose Grn. Cres. EH21 —1F **19**
Goose Grn. Pl. EH21 —1F **19**
Goose Grn. Rd. EH21 —1F **19**
Gordon Av. EH19 —7J **31**
Gordon Ct. EH6 —6F **9**
Gordon Loan. EH12 —4G **13**
Gordon Rd. EH12 —4G **13**
Gordon St. EH6 —6F **9**
Gordon St. EH22 —6H **33**
Gordon Ter. EH16 —2A **26**
Gore Av. EH23 —6H **35**
Gorgie Cotts. EH11 —7A **14**
Gorgie Rd. EH11 —1J **23**
Gorton Av. EH18 —6F **35**
Gorton Loan. EH24 —7F **35**
Gorton Pl. EH24 —7F **35**
Gorton Rd. EH24 —7F **35**
Gorton Wlk. EH24 —7F **35**
Goschen Ho. EH10 —7E 14
(off Blantyre Ter.)
Gosford Pl. EH6 —5C **8**
Gosford Rd. EH32 —1A **20**

Gosford Wlk. EH32 —1A **20**
(off Gosford Rd.)
Gospel Wynd. EH18 —4K **31**
Gote La. EH30 —5B **4**
Gowkshill Farm Cotts. EH23
—3G **35**
Gracefield Ct. EH21 —2D **18**
Gracemount Av. EH16 —5B **26**
Gracemount Dri. EH16
—6B **26**
Gracemount Pl. EH16 —6B **26**
Gracemount Rd. EH16
—7A **26**
Gracemount Sq. EH16 —6B **26**
Graham's Rd. EH26 —2E **34**
Graham St. EH6 —5D **8**
Granby Rd. EH16 —1K **25**
Grandfield. EH6 —5B **8**
Granville. EH6 —4B **8**
Grange Ct. EH9 —6J **15**
(off Causewayside)
Grange Cres. EH9 —7H **15**
Grange Cres. E. EH32 —3D **20**
Grange Cres. W. EH32
—3D **20**
Grange Gro. EH32 —3D **20**
Grange Loan. EH9 —7G **15**
Grange Loan Gdns. EH9
—7H **15**
Grange Rd. EH9 —6H **15**
Grange Rd. EH32 —3D **20**
Grange Ter. EH9 —1H **25**
Grannies Pk. Ind. Est. EH22
—1F **33**
Grant Av. EH13 —6J **23**
Granton Cres. EH5 —4H **7**
Granton Gdns. EH5 —4J **7**
Granton Gro. EH5 —4J **7**
Granton Mains Av. EH4 —4F **7**
Granton Mains Bank. EH4
—4F **7**
Granton Mains Brae. EH4
—5F **7**
Granton Mains Ct. EH4 —5G **7**
Granton Mains Gait. EH4
—4F **7**
Granton Mains Vale. EH4
—5F **7**
Granton Mains Wynd. EH4
—4F **7**
Granton Medway. EH5 —4H **7**
Granton Pk. Av. EH5 —3H **7**
Granton Pl. EH5 —4J **7**
Granton Rd. EH5 —4J **7**
Granton Sq. EH5 —3J **7**
Granton Ter. EH5 —4J **7**
Granton View. EH5 —4J **7**
Grantully Pl. EH9 —7K **15**
Granville Ter. EH10 —6E **14**
Grassmarket. EH1
—4G **15** (5D **2**)
Gray's Ct. EH8 —4J **15** (6G **3**)
Graysknowe. EH14 —2K **23**
(off Inglis Grn. Rd.)
Grays Loan. EH10 —7D **14**
Gt. Cannon Bank. EH15
—2G **17**
Gt. Carleton Pl. EH16 —1G **27**
Gt. Carleton Sq. EH16 —1G **27**
Gt. Junction St. EH6 —5E **8**
Gt. King St. EH3
—2G **15** (1C **2**)
Gt. Michael Clo. EH6 —3C **8**
Gt. Michael Rise. EH6 —4C **8**
Gt. Stuart St. EH3 —3E **14**
Greenbank Av. EH10 —3E **24**
Greenbank Cres. EH10
—5D **24**
Greenbank Dri. EH10 —4C **24**
Greenbank Gdns. EH10
—4D **24**
Greenbank Gro. EH10 —4D **24**
Greenbank La. EH10 —3D **24**
Greenbank Loan. EH10
—4D **24**
Greenbank Pk. EH10 —4D **24**
Greenbank Pl. EH10 —3E **24**
Greenbank Rise. EH10
—4D **24**
Greenbank Rd. EH10 —4D **24**

Greenbank Row. EH10
—4D **24**
Greenbank Ter. EH10 —3E **24**
Greendykes Av. EH16 —1F **27**
Greendykes Dri. EH16 —1F **27**
Greendykes Gdns. EH16
—1F **27**
Greendykes Ho. EH16 —1F **27**
Greendykes Loan. EH16
—1F **27**
Greendykes Rd. EH16
—1E **26**
Greendykes Ter. EH16
—1F **27**
Greenend Dri. EH17 —4C **26**
Greenend Gdns. EH17 —5C **26**
Greenend Gro. EH17 —4C **26**
Greenfield Cres. EH4 —5E **28**
Greenfield Pk. EH21 —5D **18**
Greenfield Rd. EH14 —5A **28**
Greenhall Cres. EH23 —5H **35**
Greenhall Rd. EH23 —5H **35**
Greenhill Gdns. EH10 —6F **15**
Greenhill Pk. EH10 —7F **15**
Greenhill Pk. EH26 —6A **34**
Greenhill Pl. EH10 —7F **15**
Greenhill Ter. EH10 —6F **15**
Greenlaw Gro. EH26 —2D **34**
Greenlaw Hedge. EH13
—4C **24**
Greenlaw Rig. EH13 —4C **24**
Greenmantle Loan. FH16
—3B **26**
Greenside End. EH1 —1G **3**
Greenside La. EH1
—2J **15** (1G **3**)
Greenside Pl. EH1 —1G **3**
Greenside Pl. EH24 —7F **35**
Greenside Row. EH1
—2J **15** (2G **3**)
Green St. EH7 —1H **15**
Green, The. EH4 —6C **6**
Green, The. EH14 —5F **29**
Greenway, The. EH14 —4F **23**
Greyfriars Pl. EH1 —5E **2**
Grierson Av. EH5 —4K **7**
Grierson Cres. EH5 —4K **7**
Grierson Gdns. EH6 —4K **7**
Grierson Rd. EH5 —4J **7**
Grierson Sq. EH5 —4K **7**
Grierson Vs. EH5 —4K **7**
Grieve Ct. EH26 —4C **34**
Grigor Av. EH4 —7G **7**
Grigor Dri. EH4 —7G **7**
Grigor Gdns. EH4 —7H **7**
Grigor Ter. EH4 —7G **7**
Grindlay St. EH3
—4F **15** (5B **2**)
Grindlay St. Ct. EH3
—4F **15** (6B **2**)
Groathill Av. EH4 —1A **14**
Groathill Gdns. E. EH4
—1A **14**
Groathill Gdns. W. EH4
—1A **14**
Groathill Rd. N. EH4 —6F **7**
Groathill Rd. S. EH4 —1A **14**
Grosvenor Cres. EH12 —4D **14**
Grosvenor Gdns. EH12
—4D **14**
Grosvenor St. EH12 —4E **14**
Grove End. EH18 —5A **32**
Grove Pl. EH14 —6F **23**
Grove St. EH3 —4E **14**
Grove St. EH21 —3F **19**
Grove Ter. EH3 —4E **14**
Grove, The. EH21 —3G **19**
Grundieswell Rd. EH17
—6E **26**
Guardianswood. EH12
—4A **14**
Gullan's Clo. EH8
(in two parts) —3J **15** (4G **3**)
Gunnet Ct. EH4 —5D **6**
Guthrie St. EH1 —4H **15** (5F **3**)
Gyle Av. EH12 —5B **12**
Gylemuir Rd. EH12 —5E **12**
Gyle Pk. Gdns. EH12 —5C **12**
Gyle Service La. EH12
—5B **12**

Gyle Shopping Cen. EH12
—6B **12**

Haddington Pl. EH7 —1J **15**
Haddington Rd. EH21 —2J **19**
Haddington Rd. EH33 —6J **21**
Haddon's Ct. EH8 —6G **3**
Hailes App. EH13 —5J **23**
Hailes Av. EH13 —5J **23**
Hailes Bank. EH13 —5J **23**
Hailes Cres. EH13 —5J **23**
Hailes Gdns. EH13 —5H **23**
Hailes Gro. EH13 —5J **23**
Hailesland Gdns. EH14
—3E **14**
Hailesland Gro. EH14 —3G **23**
Hailesland Pk. EH14 —3G **23**
Hailesland Pl. EH14 —3G **23**
Hailesland Rd. EH14 —3F **23**
Hailes Pk. EH13 —5H **23**
Hailes St. EH3 —5F **15**
Hailes Ter. EH13 —5J **23**
Hainburn Pk. EH10 —7D **24**
Hallcroft Clo. EH28 —7A **10**
Hallcroft Cres. EH28 —7A **10**
Hallcroft Gdns. EH28 —7A **10**
Hallcroft Grn. EH28 —7A **10**
Hallcroft Neuk. EH28 —7A **10**
Hallcroft Pk. EH28 —7A **10**
Hallcroft Rise. EH28 —7A **10**
Hall Ter. EH12 —5G **13**
(off Corstorphine High St.)
Hallyards Cotts. EH29 —3B **10**
Hallyards Rd. EH29 —3B **10**
Halmyre St. EH6 —7E **8**
Hamburgh Pl. EH6 —4D **8**
Hamilton Cres. EH22 —7G **33**
Hamilton Dri. EH15 —4F **17**
Hamilton Dri. W. EH15 —4F **17**
Hamilton Gdns. EH15 —4F **17**
Hamilton Gro. EH15 —4F **17**
Hamilton Pk. EH15 —3F **17**
Hamilton Pl. EH3 —1F **15**
Hamilton's Clo. EH30 —5C **4**
Hamilton Ter. EH15 —3G **17**
Hamilton Wynd. EH6 —4D **8**
Hampton Pl. EH12 —4C **14**
Hampton Ter. EH12 —4C **14**
Hanover St. EH2
—2G **15** (2D **2**)
Harbour La. EH30 —5B **4**
Harbour Pl. EH15 —2G **17**
Harbour Rd. EH15 —2G **17**
Harbour Rd. EH21 —2C **18**
Hardengreen Farm Cotts. EH22
—5D **32**
Hardengreen Ind. Est. EH22
—4D **32**
Hardengreen Junction. EH22
—6D **32**
Harden Pl. EH11 —6D **14**
Hardwell Clo. EH8
—4J **15** (6H **3**)
Harelaw Rd. EH13 —6J **23**
Hares Clo. EH32 —2C **20**
Harewood Cres. EH16 —7E **16**
Harewood Dri. EH16 —7E **16**
Harewood Rd. EH16 —7E **16**
Harkenburn Gdns. EH26
—5A **34**
Harkness Cres. EH33 —6H **21**
Harlaw Gro. EH26 —6A **34**
Harlaw Hill. EH32 —2D **20**
Harlawhill Gdns. EH32 —2E **20**
Harlaw March. EH14 —5F **29**
Harlaw Rd. EH14 —4E **28**
Harper's Brae. EH26 —5A **34**
Harrison Gdns. EH11 —7C **14**
Harrison La. EH11 —6D **14**
Harrison Pl. EH11 —7C **14**
Harrison Rd. EH11 —6C **14**
Hartington Gdns. EH10
—6E **14**
Hartington Pl. EH10 —6E **14**
Hart St. EH1 —1H **15**
Harvest Dri. EH28 —6B **10**
Harvest Rd. EH28 —6A **10**
Harvieston Vs. EH23 —7J **35**

Hastie's Clo. EH1 —5F **3**
Hatton Pl. EH9 —6H **15**
Haugh Pk. EH14 —2J **23**
Haugh St. EH4 —1F **15**
Hawes Brae. EH30 —5D **4**
Hawkhead Cres. EH16 —4A **26**
Hawkhead Gro. EH16 —5A **26**
Hawkhill Av. EH7 —7F **9**
Hawkhill Ct. EH7 —7G **9**
Hawkins Ter. EH26 —3E **34**
Hawmuirside. EH14 —3K **23**
Hawthorn Bank. EH30 —5B **4**
Hawthornbank. EH32 —1A **20**
Hawthornbank La. EH4
—3E **14**
Hawthornbank Pl. EH6 —4C **8**
Hawthornbank Ter. EH6
—4D **8**
Hawthorn Bldgs. EH4 —3E **14**
(off Hawthornbank La.)
Hawthorn Cres. EH22 —5J **33**
Hawthornden Av. EH19
—7K **31**
Hawthornden Gdns. EH19
—4K **31**
Hawthornden Pl. EH7 —7D **8**
Hawthorn Gdns. EH20 —4E **30**
Hawthorn Pl. EH17 —6E **26**
Hawthorn Rd. EH32 —3F **21**
Hawthorn Ter. EH4 —3E **14**
Hawthorn Ter. EH32 —1F **21**
Hawthornvale. EH6 —4C **8**
Hay Av. EH16 —7F **17**
Hay Dri. EH16 —7G **17**
Hayfield. EH12 —3C **12**
Haymarket. EH12 —4E **14**
Haymarket Ter. EH12 —4D **14**
Hay Pl. EH16 —7F **17**
Hay Rd. EH16 —7F **17**
Hay Ter. EH16 —7F **17**
Hazelbank Ter. EH11 —7C **14**
Hazeldean Ter. EH16 —2B **26**
Hazel Dri. EH19 —7A **32**
Hazel La. EH20 — 6B **30**
Hazelwood Gro. EH16 —2C **26**
Headrigg Row. EH16 —3R **26**
Hedge Row. EH20 —6B **30**
Henderland Rd. EH12 —4B **14**
Henderson Gdns. EH6 —5E **8**
Henderson Gdns. EH33
—6H **21**
Henderson Pl. EH3 —1G **15**
Henderson Pl. La. EH3
—1G **15**
Henderson Row. EH3 —1F **15**
Henderson St. EH6 —5E **8**
Henderson Ter. EH11 —6D **14**
Henry Pl. EH6 —5K **15**
Henry Ross Pl. EH30 —5B **4**
Henry St. EH6 —5K **15**
Hepburn Dri. EH22 —3H **33**
Hercus Loan. EH21 —2D **18**
(in two parts)
Herd Ter. EH20 —6D **30**
Heriot Bri. EH1 —4G **15** (5D **2**)
Heriot Cross. EH1
—4G **15** (5D **2**)
Heriot Hill Ter. EH7 —7B **8**
Heriot Mt. EH8 —4J **15** (6H **3**)
Heriot Pl. EH3 —4G **15** (6D **2**)
Heriot Row. EH3
—2F **15** (2B **2**)
Hermand Cres. EH11 —7C **14**
Hermand St. EH11 —7B **14**
Hermand Ter. EH11 —7B **14**
Hermiston Ct. EH11 —2F **23**
(off Sighthill Bank)
Hermiston Wlk. EH14 —4B **22**
Hermitage Dri. EH10 —3F **25**
Hermitage Gdns. EH10
—3F **25**
Hermitage Pk. EH6 —7G **9**
Hermitage Pk. Gro. EH6
—7G **9**
Hermitage Pk. S. EH6 —7G **9**
Hermitage Pl. EH6 —6F **9**
Hermitage Ter. EH10 —2F **25**
Herwit St. EH5 —2H **7**
Hough, The. EH33 —5G **21**
(in two parts)

Higginson Loan. EH22
—1K **35**
High Buckstone. EH10
—6G **25**
Highlea Circ. EH14 —6D **28**
Highlea Gro. EH14 —5D **28**
High Pk. Rise. EH26 —7C **34**
High Riggs. EH3
—4F **15** (6B **2**)
High School Yards. EH1
—4J **15** (5G **3**)
High St. Bonnyrigg, EH19
—5A **32**
High St. Cockenzie, EH32
—1A **20**
High St. Dalkeith, EH22
—2F **33**
High St. Edinburgh, EH1
—3H **15** (4E **2**)
High St. Kirkliston, EH29
—2B **10**
High St. Lasswade, EH18
—4K **31**
High St. Loanhead, EH20
—6F **31**
High St. Musselburgh, EH21
—2E **18**
High St. Penicuik, EH26
—7C **34**
High St. Prestonpans, EH32
—3C **20**
High St. S. Queensferry, EH30
—5B **4**
High St. Tranent, EH33
—6G **21**
High Way, The. FH8 —3E **16**
Hillcoat Loan. EH15 —2G **17**
Hillcoat Pl. EH15 —2G **17**
Hill Ct. EH30 —5B **4**
Hillend Pl. EH8 —2C **16**
(off London Rd.)
Hill Head. EH19 —5A **32**
Hillhouse Rd. EH4 —7C **6**
Hillpark Av. EH4 —7C **6**
Hillpark Brae. EH4 —2H **13**
Hillpark Ct. EH4 —7C **6**
Hillpark Cres. EH4 — 1H **13**
Hillpark Dri. EH4 —7C **6**
Hillpark Gdns. EH4 —1H **13**
Hillpark Grn. EH4 —1H **13**
Hillpark Gro. EH4 —1H **13**
Hillpark Loan. EH4 —1J **13**
Hillpark Rd. EH4 —1H **13**
Hillpark Ter. EH4 —1H **13**
Hillpark Way. EH4 —1J **13**
Hillpark Wood. EH4 —1J **13**
Hill Pl. EH8 —4J **15** (6G **3**)
Hill Pl. EH22 —1K **35**
Hillside Cres. EH7 —1J **15**
Hillside Cres. N. EH23
—6J **35**
Hillside Cres. S. EH23 —6J **35**
Hillside St. EH7 —1K **15**
Hill Sq. EH8 —5G **3**
Hill St. EH2 —2F **15** (2B **2**)
Hill St. La. N. EH2
—2F **15** (2B **2**)
Hill St. La. S. EH2
—3F **15** (3B **2**)
Hilltown Ter. EH22 —3J **27**
Hillview. EH4 —1K **13**
Hill View. EH26 —6D **34**
Hillview Cotts. EH28 —7B **10**
Hillview Cres. EH12 —4F **13**
Hillview Dri. EH12 —4E **12**
Hillview Gdns. EH20 —6C **30**
Hillview Rd. EH12 —4E **12**
Hillview Ter. EH12 —4E **12**
Hillwood Av. EH28 —6C **10**
Hillwood Cres. EH28 —6C **10**
Hillwood Gdns. EH28 —5C **10**
Hillwood Pl. EH30 —5B **4**
Hillwood Rise. EH28 —6C **10**
Hillwood Rd. EH28 —6C **10**
Hillwood Ter. EH28 —6C **10**
Hogarth Av. EH23 —6G **35**
Holly Bank. EH22 —6K **33**
Hollybank Ter. EH11 —7C **14**
Holly Ter. EH19 —7A **32**
Holly Wlk. EH20 —6B **30**

Holyrood Ct. EH8
—3K **15** (4J **3**)
Holyrood Pk. Rd. EH16
—6K **15**
Holyrood Rd. EH8
—3J **15** (4H **3**)
Home St. EH3 —5F **15** (7B **2**)
Hopefield Rd. EH19 —7K **31**
Hopefield Pl. EH19 —7K **31**
Hopefield Ter. EH6 —4D **8**
Hopefield Ter. EH19 —7K **31**
Hope La. EH15 —3H **17**
(in three parts)
Hope Pk. Cres. EH8 —5J **15**
Hope Pk. Sq. EH8
—5J **15** (7G **3**)
Hope Pk. Ter. EH8 —5J **15**
Hope Pl. FH21 —1H **19**
Hope Pl. EH33 —5G **21**
Hope St. EH2 —3F **15** (3A **2**)
Hope St. EH30 —6B **4**
Hope St. La. EH2
—3F **15** (4A **2**)
Hope Ter. EH9 —7G **15**
Hopetoun Cres. EH7 —1J **15**
Hopetoun Cres. La. EH7
—1J **15**
Hopetoun Rd. EH30 —5A **4**
Hopetoun St. EH7 —1J **15**
Horne Ter. EH11 —5E **14**
Horsburgh Bank. EH14
—2E **28**
Horsburgh Gdns. EH14
—2E **28**
Horsburgh Gro. EH14 —2E **28**
Horse Wynd. EH8
—3K **15** (3K **3**)
Hoseason Gdns. EH4 —2F **13**
Hosie Rigg. EH15 —6H **17**
House o'Hill Av. EH4 —7D **6**
House o'Hill Brae. EH4 —7D **6**
House o'Hill Cres. EH4 —7D **6**
House o'Hill Gdns. EH4 —7E **6**
House o'Hill Grn. EH4 —7D **6**
House o'Hill Gro. EH4 —7D **6**
House o'Hill Pl. EH4 —7D **6**
House o'Hill Rd. EH4 —7D **6**
House o'Hill Row. EH4 —7E **6**
House o'Hill Ter. EH4 —1K **13**
Howard Pl. EH3 —7B **8**
Howard St. EH3 —7B **8**
Howden Hall Cotts. EH16
—6A **26**
Howden Hall Ct. EH16 —6K **25**
Howden Hall Cres. EH16
—7K **25**
Howden Hall Dri. EH16
—6K **25**
Howden Hall Gdns. EH16
—6A **26**
Howden Hall Loan. EH16
—6K **25**
Howden Hall Pk. EH16
—6K **25**
Howden Hall Rd. EH16
—6A **26**
Howden Hall Way. EH16
—7A **26**
Howden St. EH8
—5J **15** (6G **3**)
Howe Pk. EH10 —7D **24**
Howe St. EH3 —2G **15** (1C **2**)
Hughes Cres. EH22 —7K **33**
Hugh Miller Pl. EH3 —1F **15**
Hugh Russell Pl. EH30 —6B **4**
Humbie Rd. EH29 —1A **10**
Hungerage Sq. EH33 —7H **21**
Hunt Clo. EH22 —1F **33**
Hunter Av. EH20 —5G **31**
Hunter Ct. EH20 —5G **31**
Hunterfield Ct. EH23 —6J **35**
Hunterfield Rd. EH23 —5H **35**
Hunterfield Ter. EH23 —5G **35**
Hunter's Clo. EH1 —5D **2**
Hunter's Hill. EH22 —7K **33**
Hunter Sq. EH1 —3H **15** (4F **3**)
Hunter Sq. EH23 —7J **35**
Hunter Ter. EH19 —6A **32**
Hunter Ter. EH20 —5G **31**

Huntly St. EH3 —7B **8**
Hursted Av. EH22 —6J **33**
Hutchison Av. EH14 —1A **24**
Hutchison Cotts. EH14
—1A **24**
Hutchison Crossway. EH14
—7A **14**
Hutchison Gdns. EH14
—1A **24**
Hutchison Gro. EH14 —1B **24**
Hutchison Ho. EH14 —7B **14**
Hutchison Loan. EH14
—1A **24**
Hutchison Medway. EH14
—1A **24**
Hutchison Pk. EH14 —1A **24**
Hutchison Pl. EH14 —1A **24**
Hutchison Rd. EH14 —1A **24**
Hutchison Ter. EH14 —1A **24**
Hutchison View. EH14
—7A **14**
Hyndford's Clo. EH1 —4G **3**
Hyvot Av. EH17 —6D **26**
Hyvot Ct. EH17 —7D **26**
Hyvot Gdns. EH17 —6D **26**
Hyvot Grn. EH17 —7D **26**
Hyvot Gro. EH17 —6D **26**
Hyvot Loan. EH17 —5C **26**
Hyvot Pk. EH17 —7D **26**
Hyvot's Bank Av. EH17
—6E **26**
Hyvot Ter. EH17 —6D **26**
Hyvot View. EH17 —7D **26**

Imrie Pl. EH26 —6C **34**
Inchcolm Ct. EH4 —5F **7**
Inchcolm Ter. EH30 —6B **4**
Inch Garvie Ct. EH4 —5D **6**
Inchgarvie Pk. EH30 —5A **4**
Inchkeith Av. EH30 —6C **34**
Inchkeith Ct. EH7 —7D **8**
Inchmickery Ct. EH4 —5D **6**
Inch View. EH32 —3C **20**
Inchview Cres. EH21 —7A **20**
Inchview N. EH32 —3B **20**
Inchview Rd. EH21 —3K **19**
Inchview Ter. EH7 —2F **17**
India Bldgs. EH1 —5E **2**
India Pl. EH3 —2F **15** (1A **2**)
India St. EH3 —2F **15** (1B **2**)
Industrial Rd. EH6 —6G **9**
Industry Homes. EH6 —5D **8**
Industry La. EH6 —5D **8**
Infirmary St. EH1
—4J **15** (5G **3**)
Inglewood Pl. EH16 —4B **26**
Inglis Av. EH32 —1A **20**
Inglis Grn. Rd. EH14 —2K **23**
Inglis Ct. EH1 —5D **2**
Ingliston Cotts. EH28 —4E **10**
Ingliston Rd. EH28 —4E **10**
Inkerman Ct. EH26 —3D **34**
Inveralmond Dri. EH4 —5H **5**
Inveralmond Gdns. EH4
—5H **5**
Inveralmond Gro. EH4 —5H **5**
Inveravon Rd. EH20 —4E **30**
Inveravon Ter. EH21 —3E **18**
Inveresk Brae. EH21 —3F **19**
Inveresk Ind. Est. EH21
—3E **18**
Inveresk Mills Ind. Pk. EH21
—4D **18**
Inveresk Rd. EH21 —3E **18**
Inveresk Village Rd. EH21
—4F **19**
Inverleith Av. EH3 —6A **8**
Inverleith Av. S. EH3 —6A **8**
Inverleith Gdns. EH3 —6K **7**
Inverleith Gro. EH3 —7J **7**
Inverleith Pl. EH3 —7J **7**
Inverleith Pl. La. EH3 —6A **8**
Inverleith Row. EH3 —6A **8**
Inverleith Ter. EH3 —7A **8**
Inverleith Ter. La. EH3 —7A **8**
Iona St. EH6 —7E **8**
Ironmills Rd. EH22 —2C **32**
Ironrock St. EH5 —2H **7**
Ivanhoe Cres. EH16 —3B **26**

Ivy Ter. EH11 —6C **14**

Jackson's Clo. EH1 —4F **3**
Jackson St. EH26 —6B **34**
Jamaica M. EH3 —1B **2**
Jamaica St. EH3 —2F **15**
(in two parts)
Jamaica St. N. La. EH3
—2F **15** (1B **2**)
Jamaica St. S. La. EH3
—2F **15** (1B **2**)
James Ct. EH1 —4E **2**
James Craig Wlk. EH1 —2F **3**
James Lean Av. EH22 —2G **33**
James Leary Way. EH19
—5B **32**
Jameson Pl. EH6 —7E **8**
James St. EH15 —3J **17**
James St. EH21 —2F **19**
James St. La. EH15 —3J **17**
Janefield. EH17 —1D **30**
Jane St. EH6 —6E **8**
Jane Ter. EH7 —2A **16**
Jarnac Ct. EH22 —2F **33**
(off High St. Dalkeith)
Jawbone Wlk. EH3 —5H **15**
Jean Armour Av. EH16
—3A **26**
Jean Armour Dri. EH22
—3J **33**
Jeffrey Av. EH4 —2K **13**
Jeffrey St. EH1 —3J **15** (3F **3**)
Jessfield Ter. EH6 —4C **8**
Jewel, The. EH15 —6J **17**
John Bernard Way. EH23
—7H **35**
John Cres. EH33 —6G **21**
John Humble St. EH22
—1K **35**
John Knox Pl. EH26 —6C **34**
John Mason Ct. EH30 —6C **4**
Johnnie Cope's Rd. EH32 &
(in two parts) EH33 —4E **20**
John Russel Ct. EH6 —4E **8**
(off Prince Regent St.)
Johnsburn Grn. EH14 —4D **28**
Johnsburn Haugh. EH14
—4D **28**
Johnsburn Pk. EH14 —4D **28**
Johnsburn Rd. EH14 —4D **28**
John's La. EH6 —5F **9**
John's Pl. EH6 —5F **9**
Johnston Pl. EH26 —3C **34**
Johnston Ter. EH1
—4G **15** (5C **2**)
Johnston Ter. EH32 —1B **20**
John St. EH15 —3J **17**
John St. EH26 —5B **34**
John St. La. EH15 —3J **17**
John St. La. EH26 —6B **34**
John St. La. E. EH15 —3J **17**
John St. La. W. EH15 —3J **17**
Joppa Gdns. EH15 —4J **17**
Joppa Gro. EH15 —4J **17**
Joppa Pans. EH15 —1A **18**
Joppa Pk. EH15 —4K **17**
Joppa Rd. EH15 —4J **17**
Joppa Ter. EH15 —4J **17**
Jordan La. EH10 —1F **25**
Jubilee Cres. EH23 —5H **35**
Jubilee Rd. EH12 —4F **11**
Junction Pl. EH6 —6E **8**
Juner Pl. EH23 —5H **35**
Juniper Av. EH14 —6E **22**
Juniper Gdns. EH14 —6E **22**
Juniper Gro. EH14 —6E **22**
Juniper La. EH14 —6F **23**
Juniperlee. EH14 —6F **23**
Juniper Pk. Rd. EH14 —6F **23**
Juniper Ter. EH14 —7E **22**
Juniper Ter. EH14 —6E **22**
(off Juniper La.)

Kaimes Rd. EH12 —4G **13**
Kaimes View. EH22 —5H **27**
Katesmill Rd. EH14 —4K **23**
Kay Gdns. EH32 —1A **20**
Kedslie Pl. EH16 —5K **25**

Kedslie Rd. EH16 —5K **25**
Keir Hardie Dri. EH22 —1K **35**
Keir St. EH3 —4G **15** (6D **2**)
Keith Cres. EH4 —2K **13**
Keith Ho. EH12 —7C **12**
Keith Row. EH4 —2A **14**
Keith Ter. EH4 —2K **13**
Kekewich Av. EH7 —1F **17**
Kemp Pl. EH3 —1F **15**
Kempston Pl. EH30 —6C **4**
Kenilworth Dri. EH16 —4A **26**
Kenmure Av. EH8 —3C **16**
Kenneth Mackenzie Ho. EH7
—7H **15**
Kennington Av. FH20 —6E **30**
Kennington Ter. EH20 —6E **30**
Kentigern Mall. EH26 —6C **34**
Kerr Av. EH22 —3D **32**
Kerr Rd. EH33 —6G **21**
Kerr St. EH3 —1F **15**
Kerr's Wynd. EH21 —2F **19**
Kerr Way. EH33 —7G **21**
Kevock Rd. EH18 —5J **31**
Kevock Vale Caravan Pk. EH18
—5K **31**
Kew Ter. EH12 —4C **14**
Kilchurn Ct. EH12 —4C **12**
(off Craigievar Wynd)
Kilgraston Ct. EH9 —7G **15**
Kilgraston Rd. EH9 —7H **15**
Kilmaurs Rd. EH16 —7A **16**
Kilmaurs Ter. EH16 —7A **16**
Kilncroftside. EH14 —2K **23**
Kilwinning Pl. EH21 —2E **18**
Kilwinning St. EH21 —2F **19**
Kilwinning Ter. EH21 —3F **19**
Kimmerghame Ho. EH4 —7H **7**
Kimmerghame Rd. EH22 —2J **33**
Kinellan Gdns. EH12 —4A **14**
Kinellan Rd. EH12 —3A **14**
King Edward's Way. EH29
—2A **10**
Kinghorn Pl. EH6 —5C **8**
King Malcolm Clo. EH10
—7H **25**
Kingsburgh Rd. EH12 —4A **14**
Kings Cramond. EH4 —5J **5**
Kings Ga. Junction. EH22
—1D **32**
Kings Haugh. EH16 —7C **16**
Kingsknowe Av. EH14 —4J **23**
Kingsknowe Ct. EH14 —3H **23**
Kingsknowe Cres. EH14
—3J **23**
Kingsknowe Dri. EH14 —3J **23**
Kingsknowe Gdns. EH14
—4J **23**
Kingsknowe Gro. EH14
—4J **23**
Kingsknowe Pk. EH14 —4J **23**
Kingsknowe Pl. EH14 —3H **23**
Kingsknowe Rd. N. EH14
—3J **23**
Kingsknowe Rd. S. EH14
—3J **23**
Kingsknowe Ter. EH14
—3J **23**
Kingslaw Ct. EH33 —7H **21**
King's Pl. EH15 —2G **17**
King's Rd. EH15 —2G **17**
King's Rd. EH33 —7G **21**
King's Stables La. EH1
—4G **15** (5C **2**)
King's Stables Rd. EH1
—3F **15** (4B **2**)
Kingston Av. EH16 —3C **26**
King St. EH6 —5E **8**
King St. EH21 —3F **19**
Kinleith Ind. Est. EH14 —1K **29**
Kinnaird Pk. EH15 —7J **17**
Kinnear Rd. EH3 —6J **7**
Kippielaw Dri. EH22 —3H **33**
Kippielaw Gdns. EH22 —4H **33**
Kippielaw Medway. EH22
—4H **33**
Kippielaw Pk. EH22 —5J **33**
Kippielaw Rd. EH22 —4H **33**
Kippielaw Wlk. EH22 —3H **33**
Kirk Brae. EH16 —3A **26**
Kirk Cramond. EH4 —4J **5**
Kirkgate. EH6 —5E **8**

Kirkgate. EH14 —1J **29**
Kirkgate. EH16 —5A **26**
Kirkgate Ho. EH6 —5F **9**
Kirkhill Dri. EH16 —7A **16**
Kirkhill Gdns. EH16 —6A **16**
Kirkhill Gdns. EH26 —6C **34**
Kirkhill Rd. EH16 —6A **16**
Kirkhill Rd. EH26 —6C **34**
Kirkhill Ter. EH16 —6A **16**
Kirkhill Ter. EH23 —5F **35**
Kirklands. EH12 —7F **13**
Kirklands. EH26 —6B **34**
Kirkliston Rd. EH28 —4A **10**
Kirkliston Rd. EH30 —5B **4**
Kirk Loan. EH12 —5G **13**
Kirk Pk. EH16 —4A **26**
Kirk St. EH6 —6E **8**
Kirk St. EH22 —3D **20**
Kirkstyle Gdns. EH29 —2B **10**
Kirkstyle Pl. EH29 —2A **10**
Kirkton Bank. EH26 —6A **34**
Kirkwood Pl. EH7 —2A **16**
(off Lwr. London Rd.)
Kisimul Ct. EH4 —4C **12**
Kitchener Ho. EH16 —2A **26**
(off Gordon Ter.)
Kittle Yards. EH9 —7J **15**
Klondyke St. EH21 —4A **18**
Klondyke Way. EH21 —7K **17**
Knightslaw Pl. EH26 —6A **34**
Knockill Braehead. EH14
—4J **23**
Knowetop Pl. EH25 —1A **34**
Komarom Ct. EH22 —2F **33**
(off Buccleuch St.)
Komarom Pl. EH22 —2J **33**
Kyle Pl. EH7 —2K **15** (1K **3**)

Laburnum Pl. EH22 —7K **33**
Ladehead. EH6 —6C **8**
Lade, The. EH14 —5F **29**
Ladiemeadow. EH12 —6G **13**
Lady Brae. EH23 —7J **35**
Lady Brae Pl. EH23 —6J **35**
Ladycroft. EH14 —3E **28**
Ladyfield Pl. EH3
—4F **15** (6A **2**)
Lady Lawson St. EH3
—4G **15** (5C **2**)
Lady Menzies Pl. EH7 —1A **16**
Lady Nairne Cres. EH8
—3D **16**
Lady Nairne Gro. EH8 —4D **16**
Lady Nairne Loan. EH8
—4D **16**
Lady Nairne Pl. EH8 —4D **16**
Lady Rd. EH16 —1A **26**
Lady Rd. Pl. EH22 —7G **33**
Ladysmith Rd. EH9 —2J **25**
Lady Stairs Clo. EH1 —4E **2**
Lady Victoria Bus. Cen. EH22
—3F **35**
Ladywell. EH12 —2E **18**
Ladywell Av. EH12 —5F **13**
Ladywell Ct. EH12 —5F **13**
Ladywell Gdns. EH12 —5F **13**
Ladywell Ho. EH12 —5E **12**
Ladywell Rd. EH12 —5E **12**
Ladywell Way. EH21 —2E **18**
Lady Wynd. EH1 —5C **2**
Laichfield. EH14 —1K **23**
Laichpark Loan. EH14 —1K **23**
(off Chesser Loan)
Laichpark Pl. EH14 —1K **23**
Laichpark Rd. EH14 —1K **23**
Laing Ter. EH15 —3J **17**
Laing Ter. EH26 —4C **34**
Laird Ter. EH19 —7B **32**
Lamb Ct. EH19 —6A **32**
Lamb's Clo. EH8 —5J **15**
Lambs Ct. EH6 —3B **8**
Lamb's Pend. EH26 —7C **34**
Lammermoor Gdns. EH33
—6F **21**
Lammermoor Ter. EH16
—3C **26**
Lammermoor Ter. EH33
—6F **21**

Lammerview. EH33 —7H **21**
Lampacre Rd. EH12 —5G **13**
Lanark Rd. EH13 & EH14
(Edinburgh) —5H **23**
Lanark Rd. EH14 —7F **23**
(Juniper Green)
Lanark Rd. W. EH14 —4A **28**
Lane, The. EH21 —7G **19**
Langlaw Rd. EH22 —5J **33**
Lang Loan. EH20 —3E **30**
Langloan Rd. EH17 —2E **30**
Langton Rd. EH9 —1J **25**
Lansbury Ct. EH22 —2F **33**
Lansdowne Cres. EH12
—4D **14**
Lansdowne Ho. EH12 —4B **14**
Lapicide Pl. EH6 —5D **8**
Larbourfield. EH11 —3F **23**
Larch Cres. EH22 —7K **33**
Larchfield. EH14 —3E **28**
Larchfield Neuk. EH14 —3E **28**
Largo Pl. EH6 —5D **8**
Larkfield Dri. EH22 —4C **32**
Larkfield Rd. EH22 —3D **32**
Lasswade Bank. EH17 —7C **26**
Lasswade Gro. EH17 —7C **26**
Lasswade Junction. EH17
—2H **31**
Lasswade Rd. EH16 —5B **26**
Lasswade Rd. EH17 & EH18
—7C **26**
Lasswade Rd. EH20 —5G **31**
Lasswade Rd. EH22 —3C **32**
Lauderdale St. EH9 —6G **15**
Lauder Loan. EH9 —7A **16**
Lauder Rd. EH9 —6H **15**
Lauder Rd. EH22 —3G **33**
Laundry Cotts. EH23 —5G **35**
Laurel Bank. EH22 —7K **33**
Laurelbank Pl. EH22 —7K **33**
Laurel Bank Rd. EH22 —7K **33**
Laurel Ter. EH11 —6C **14**
Laurie St. EH6 —6F **9**
Lauriston Farm Rd. EH4
—6B **6**
Lauriston Gdns. EH3
—5G **15** (6C **2**)
Lauriston Pk. EH3
—5G **15** (6C **2**)
Lauriston Pl. EH3
—4G **15** (7B **2**)
Lauriston St. EH3
—4G **15** (6C **2**)
Lauriston Ter. EH3
—4G **15** (6D **2**)
Laverockbank Av. EH5 —4B **8**
Laverockbank Cres. EH5
—4B **8**
Laverockbank Gdns. EH5
—4B **8**
Laverockbank Gro. EH5 —4B **8**
Laverockbank Rd. EH5 —4B **8**
Laverockbank Ter. EH5 —4B **8**
Laverockdale Cres. EH13
—7K **23**
Laverockdale Loan. EH13
—7K **23**
Laverockdale Pk. EH13
—7K **23**
Laverock Dri. EH26 —5A **34**
Lawers Sq. EH26 —4D **34**
Lawfield Cotts. EH22 —5K **33**
Lawfield Rd. EH22 —6J **33**
Lawhead Pl. EH26 —7A **34**
Lawnmarket. EH1
—3H **15** (4E **2**)
Law Pl. EH15 —2G **17**
Lawrie Dri. EH26 —4B **34**
Lawrie Ter. EH26 —6E **30**
Lawson Cres. EH30 —6C **4**
Leadervale Rd. EH16 —4K **25**
Leadervale Ter. EH16 —4K **25**
Leamington Pl. EH10 —5F **15**
Leamington Rd. EH3 —5E **14**
Leamington Ter. EH10 —5E **14**
Learmonth Av. EH4 —1D **14**
Learmonth Ct. EH4 —2D **14**
Learmonth Cres. EH4 —2D **14**
Learmonth Gdns. EH4
—2D **14**

Learmonth Gdns. La. EH4
—2D **14**
Learmonth Gdns. M. EH4
—1E **14**
Learmonth Gro. EH4 —1D **14**
Learmonth Pk. EH4 —1D **14**
Learmonth Pl. EH4 —1D **14**
Learmonth Ter. EH4 —2D **14**
Learmonth Ter. La. EH4
—2D **14**
Learmonth View. EH4 —2E **14**
Ledi Ter. EH26 —4D **34**
Lee Cres. EH15 —3H **17**
Leighton Cres. EH22 —6H **33**
Leith St. EH1 —2H **15** (2F **3**)
Leith Wlk. EH7 & EH6
—1J **15** (1G **3**)
Lennel Av. EH12 —3A **14**
Lennie Cotts. EH12 —3A **12**
Lennox Row. EH5 —4A **8**
Lennox St. EH4 —2E **14**
Lennox St. La. EH4 —2E **14**
Lennymuir. EH12 —2H **11**
Leslie Pl. EH4 —1F **15**
Leven Clo. EH3 —5F **15**
Leven St. EH3 —5F **15**
Leven Ter. EH3 —5G **15** (7C **2**)
Lewis Ter. EH11 —4E **14**
Lewisvale Av. EH21 —3G **19**
Lewisvale Ct. EH21 —3G **19**
Leyden Pk. EH19 —5A **32**
Leyden Pl. EH19 —6A **32**
Liberton Brae. EH16 —3A **26**
Liberton Dri. EH16 —4K **25**
Liberton Gdns. EH16 —6A **26**
Liberton Pl. EH16 —5A **26**
Liberton Rd. EH16 —3A **26**
Lidgate Shot. EH28 —1A **10**
Liddesdale Pl. EH3 —7A **8**
Lilac Av. EH22 —7K **33**
Lily Hill Ter. EH8 —2C **16**
Lily Ter. EH11 —7C **14**
Limefield. EH17 —7E **26**
Lime Gro. EH22 —7K **33**
Lime Pl. EH19 —7A **32**
Limes, The. EH10 —7E **14**
Linden Pl. EH6 —6C **9**
Linden Pl. EH20 —5G **31**
Lindores Dri. EH33 —6H **21**
Lindsay Pl. EH6 —4D **8**
Lindsay Rd. EH6 —4B **8**
Lindsay St. EH6 —4D **8**
Lingerwood Cotts. EH22
—2F **35**
Lingerwood Farm Cotts. EH22
—2G **35**
Lingerwood Rd. EH22 —2F **35**
Lingerwood Wlk. EH22
—2G **35**
Linkfield Ct. EH21 —2G **19**
Linkfield Rd. EH21 —2F **19**
Links Av. EH21 —1D **18**
Links Ct. EH32 —1B **20**
Links Gdns. EH6 —5G **9**
Links Gdns. La. EH6 —5G **9**
Links La. EH6 —5F **9**
Links Pl. EH6 —5F **9**
Links Pl. EH32 —1C **20**
Links Rd. EH32 —1B **20**
Links St. EH21 —2E **18**
Links View. EH21 —1E **18**
Links View. EH32 —1C **20**
Linksview Ho. EH6 —5F **9**
Links Wlk. EH32 —1C **20**
Linty La. EH26 —5A **34**
Lismore Av. EH8 —2C **16**
Lismore Cres. EH8 —2C **16**
Liston Dri. EH29 —1A **10**
Liston Pl. EH29 —1A **10**
Liston Rd. EH29 —2A **10**
Lit. Acre. EH22 —2G **35**
Lit. France Ho. EH17 —4D **26**
Lit. King St. EH1
—2H **15** (1F **3**)
Little Rd. EH16 —5A **26**
Livesay Ter. EH26 —3D **34**
Livingstone Pl. EH9 —6H **15**
Lixmount Av. EH5 —4B **8**
Lixmount Gdns. EH5 —4B **8**
Loanburn. EH26 —6B **34**

Loanburn Av. EH26 —6C **34**
Loanhead Rd. EH20 —3D **30**
Loaning Cres. EH7 —1D **16**
Loaning Rd. EH7 —1C **16**
Loanstone Cotts. EH26
—6E **34**
Loan, The. EH20 —5F **31**
Loan, The. EH30 —5B **4**
Lochend Av. EH7 —7G **9**
Lochend Castle Barns. EH7
—1B **16**
Lochend Cres. EH7 —1C **16**
Lochend Dri. EH7 —1B **16**
Lochend Gdns. EH7 —1B **16**
Lochend Gro. EH7 —1C **16**
Lochend Ho. EH7 —1C **16**
Lochend Ind. Est. EH28
(in three parts) —5B **10**
Lochend Pk. EH7 —1B **16**
Lochend Quadrant. EH7
—1C **16**
Lochend Rd. EH6 & EH7
—6F **9**
Lochend Rd. EH29 & EH28
—3A **10**
Lochend Rd. N. EH21 —2D **18**
Lochend Rd. S. EH7 —7G **9**
Lochend Rd. S. EH21 —2D **18**
Lochend Sq. EH7 —1B **16**
Loch Pl. EH30 —5B **4**
Loch Rd. EH4
—5F **15** (7B **2**)
Lochrin Pl. EH3 —5F **15** (7B **2**)
Lochrin Pl. La. EH3
—5F **15** (7A **2**)
Lochrin Ter. EH3 —7B **2**
Loch Rd. EH4 —1J **13**
Loch Rd. EH30 —5B **4**
Loch Rd. EH33 —6H **21**
Lochview Ct. EH8
—3K **15** (4J **3**)
Lockerby Cotts. EH16 —6C **26**
Lockerby Cres. EH16 —6C **26**
Lockerby Gro. EH16 —6C **26**
Lockharton Av. EH14 —2B **24**
Lockharton Cres. EH14
—2C **24**
Lockharton Gdns. EH14
—1C **24**
Lockhart Ter. EH25 —1A **34**
Loganlea Av. EH7 —1D **16**
Loganlea Dri. EH7 —2C **16**
Loganlea Gdns. EH7 —1C **16**
Loganlea Loan. EH7 —1C **16**
Loganlea Pl. EH7 —2D **16**
Loganlea Rd. EH7 —1D **16**
Loganlea Ter. EH7 —1D **16**
Logan St. EH3 —1G **15**
Logie Grn. Gdns. EH7 —7B **8**
Logie Grn. Loan. EH7 —7B **8**
Logie Grn. Rd. EH7 —7B **8**
Logie Mill. EH7 —7B **8**
Lomond Rd. EH5 —4A **8**
Lomond Vale. EH26 —4D **34**
Lomond Wlk. EH20 —4C **30**
London Rd. EH7 & EH8
—2J **15**
London St. EH3 —1H **15**
Long Craigs. EH32 —1J **21**
Long Crook. EH30 —6A **4**
Long Dalmahoy Rd. EH27 &
EH28 —1A **28**
Longdykes. EH32 —2E **20**
Longdykes Rd. EH32 —2F **21**
Longformacus Rd. EH16
—5A **26**
Longstone Av. EH14 —2J **23**
Longstone Cotts. EH14
—2J **23**
Longstone Cres. EH14 —1J **23**
Longstone Gdns. EH14
—1H **23**
Longstone Gro. EH14 —2J **23**
Longstone Pk. EH14 —2J **23**
Longstone Rd. EH14 —2J **23**
Longstone St. EH14 —2J **23**
Longstone Ter. EH14 —1H **23**

Longstone View. EH14
—1H **23**
Lonsdale Ter. EH3
—5G **15** (7C **2**)
*Lord Russell Pl. EH9 —6J **15***
(off Causewayside)
Loretto Ct. EH21 —4D **18**
Lorne Grn. EH20 —4D **30**
Lorne Ho. EH3 —3E **14**
Lorne Pl. EH6 —7E **8**
Lorne Sq. EH6 —7E **8**
Lorne St. EH6 —7E **8**
Lothian Bank. EH22 —4E **32**
Lothian Dri. EH22 —5H **33**
Lothian Rd. EH1 & EH3
—3F **15** (4A **2**)
Lothian Rd. EH22 —2F **33**
Lothian St. EH1 —4H **15** (6F **3**)
Lothian St. EH19 —6A **32**
Lothian St. EH22 —2F **33**
Lothian St. EH24 —7F **35**
Lothian Ter. EH22 —2G **35**
Louisa Sq. EH24 —7F **35**
Lovedale Av. EH14 —4D **28**
Lovedale Cres. EH14 —4E **28**
Lovedale Gdns. EH14 —4E **28**
Lovedale Gro. EH14 —4D **28**
Lovedale Rd. EH14 —4E **28**
Lover's La. EH30 —6C **4**
(in two parts)
Lovers Loan. EH9 —6H **15**
Lwr. Broomieknowe. EH18
—5K **31**
Lwr. Gilmore Pl. EH3 —5F **15**
Lwr. Granton Rd. EH5 —4A **8**
Lwr. Joppa Ter. EH15 —3J **17**
Lwr. London Rd. EH7 —2A **16**
Lowrie Av. EH26 —7A **34**
Lowrie's Den Rd. EH26
—7A **34**
Lugton Brae. EH22 —1E **32**
Lumsden Ct. EH28 —7B **10**
Lussielaw Rd. EH9 —2K **25**
Lutton Pl. EH8 —5J **15**
Lygon Rd. EH16 —2K **25**
Lyndene Sq. EH20 —4C **30**
Lynedoch Pl. EH3 —3E **14**
Lynedoch Pl. La. EH3 —3E **14**
Lyne St. EH7 —2A **16**
Lyne Ter. EH26 —4D **34**
Lyon's Clo. EH1 —4F **3**

Macbeth Moir Rd. EH21
—2J **19**
McCathie Dri. EH22 —7G **33**
MacCormick Ter. EH26
—3C **34**
McDiarmid Gro. EH22 —2G **35**
McDonald Pl. EH7 —7C **8**
McDonald Rd. EH7 —7C **8**
McDonald St. EH7 —7D **8**
Macdowall Rd. EH9 —1J **25**
McGahey Ct. EH22 —2G **35**
McKelvie Pde. EH5 —3A **8**
Mackenzie Pl. EH3 —2E **14**
*Mackies Way. EH32 —3C **20***
(off Inch View)
McKinlay Ter. EH20 —6D **30**
McKinnon Dri. EH7 —3K **15**
McLaren Rd. EH9 —7A **16**
McLaren Ter. EH11 —4E **14**
McLean Pl. EH18 —7H **31**
McLean Pl. EH23 —5J **35**
McLean Wlk. EH22 —2G **35**
McLeod Cres. EH32 —3D **20**
McLeod St. EH11 —5C **14**
McNeill Av. EH20 —5E **30**
McNeill Path. EH33 —6G **21**
McNeill Pl. EH20 —5E **30**
McNeill St. EH11 —5F **15**
McNeill Ter. EH20 —5D **30**
McNeill Wlk. EH33 —7G **21**
McNeill Way. EH33 —7G **21**
McPhail Sq. EH33 —6H **21**
McQuade St. EH19 —5C **32**
Mactaggart Loan. EH22
—2G **35**
Madeira Pl. EH6 —5D **8**
Madeira St. EH6 —4D **8**

Maesterton Pl. EH22 —2G **35**
Magdala Cres. EH12 —4D **14**
Magdala M. EH12 —4D **14**
Magdalene Av. EH15 —5H **17**
Magdalene Cotts. EH21
—1B **18**
Magdalene Ct. EH15 —5H **17**
Magdalene Dri. EH15 —5G **17**
Magdalene Gdns. EH15
—5H **17**
Magdalene Loan. EH15
—5H **17**
Magdalene Medway. EH15
—5H **17**
Magdalene Pl. EH15 —5H **17**
Maidencraig Ct. EH4 —2A **14**
Maidencraig Cres. EH4
—1A **14**
Maidencraig Gro. EH4 —1A **14**
Main Point. EH3 —6C **2**
Mains of Craigmillar. EH16
—2D **26**
Main St. EH4 —7C **6**
Main St. EH6 —4B **8**
Main St. EH14 —3E **28**
Main St. EH22 —1F **35**
Main St. EH23 —7H **35**
Main St. EH25 —1A **34**
Main St. EH28 —7B **10**
Main St. EH29 —1A **10**
Main St. EH30 —7E **4**
Maitland Av. EH21 —2C **18**
Maitland Hog La. EH29
—2A **10**
Maitland Pk. Rd. EH21
—2C **18**
Maitland St. EH21 —2C **18**
Malcolm Ho. EH4 —6J **7**
Mall Av. EH21 —2E **18**
Malleny Av. EH14 —4E **28**
Malleny Millgate. EH14
—5F **29**
Malta Grn. EH4 —1F **15**
Malta Ter. EH4 —1F **15**
Mandoroton Ct. EH6 —6F **9**
Manderston St. EH6 —6E **8**
Mannering Pl. EH16 —4B **26**
Manor Pl. EH3 —3E **14**
Manse La. EH32 —1A **20**
Manse Rd. EH12 —5F **13**
Manse Rd. EH25 —1B **34**
Manse Rd. EH29 —2A **10**
Manse St. EH12 —5F **13**
Mansfield Av. EH21 —2E **18**
Mansfield Av. EH22 —7G **33**
Mansfield Ct. EH21 —3F **19**
Mansfield Pl. EH3 —1H **15**
Mansfield Pl. EH22 —7G **33**
Mansfield Rd. EH14 —4E **28**
Mansfield Rd. EH21 —2E **18**
Mansionhouse Rd. EH9
—6H **15**
Marchbank Dri. EH14 —5E **28**
Marchbank Gdns. EH14
—5E **28**
Marchbank Gro. EH14 —5E **28**
Marchbank Pl. EH14 —5E **28**
Marchbank Way. EH14
—4E **28**
Marchburn Dri. EH26 —7A **34**
Marchfield Gro. EH4 —7D **6**
Marchfield Pk. EH4 —7C **6**
Marchfield Pk. La. EH4 —7C **6**
Marchfield Ter. EH4 —1J **13**
March Gro. EH4 —1J **13**
Marchhall Cres. EH16 —6A **16**
Marchhall Pl. EH16 —6A **16**
Marchhall Rd. EH16 —6A **16**
Marchmont Cres. EH9 —6H **15**
Marchmont Rd. EH9 —6G **15**
Marchmont St. EH9 —6G **15**
March Pines. EH4 —1H **13**
March Rd. EH4 —1H **13**
Mardale Cres. EH10 —7E **14**
Marine Dri. EH4 & EH5 —6J **7**
Marine Esplanade. EH6 —5H **9**
Marionville Av. EH7 —1B **16**

Marionville Cres. EH7 —1C **16**
Marionville Dri. EH7 —1C **16**
Marionville Gro. EH7 —1C **16**
Marionville Medway. EH7
    —1C **16**
Marionville Pk. EH7 —1B **16**
Marionville Rd. EH7 —2A **16**
Marischal Pl. EH4 —2A **14**
Maritime La. FH6 —5F **9**
Maritime St. EH6 —5F **9**
Market Pl. EH22 —2F **33**
Market St. EH1 —3H **15** (4E **2**)
Market St. EH21 —2D **18**
Marlborough St. EH15
    —3H **17**
Marmion Av. EH25 —1A **34**
Marmion Cres. EH16 —2B **26**
Marshall Pl. EH4 —5C **6**
Marshall Pl. EH7 —2A **16**
(off Lwr. London Rd.)
Marshall Rd. EH29 —2A **10**
Marshall's Ct. EH1
    —2J **15** (1G **3**)
Marshall St. EH8
    —4H **15** (6F **3**)
Marshall St. EH32 —1A **20**
Martello Ct. EH4 —5D **6**
Martin Gro. EH19 —5C **32**
Martin Pl. EH22 —3D **32**
Maryburn Rd. EH22 —5H **33**
Maryfield. EH7 —1K **15** (1K **3**)
Maryfield. EH15 —2H **17**
Maryfield Pl. EH7 —1A **16**
Maryfield Pl. EH19 —6B **32**
*Mary's Pl. EH4 —1E **14***
(off Raeburn Pl.)
Mary Tree Ho. EH17 —4D **26**
Mason Pl. EH18 —7J **31**
Masson Hall. EH9 —7J **15**
Maulsford Av. EH22 —5H **27**
Maurice Pl. EH9 —2H **25**
Mauricewood Av. EH26
    —4C **34**
Mauricewood Bank. EH26
    —4C **34**
Mauricewood Gro. EH26
    —4C **34**
Mauricewood Pk. EH26
    —4C **34**
Mauricewood Rise. EH26
    —4C **34**
Mauricewood Rd. EH26
    —2B **34**
Mavisbank. EH20 —6F **31**
Mavisbank Pl. EH18 —7H **31**
Maxton Ct. EH22 —2F **33**
Maxwell St. EH10 —1E **24**
Maybank Vs. EH12 —4F **13**
Mayburn Av. EH20 —5E **30**
Mayburn Bank. EH20 —5E **30**
Mayburn Ct. EH20 —5E **30**
Mayburn Cres. EH20 —4E **30**
Mayburn Dri. EH20 —5E **30**
Mayburn Gdns. EH20 —5E **30**
Mayburn Gro. EH20 —5E **30**
Mayburn Hill. EH20 —5E **30**
Mayburn Loan. EH20 —4E **30**
Mayburn Ter. EH20 —5D **30**
Mayburn Vale. EH20 —5D **30**
Mayburn Wlk. EH20 —5E **30**
Maybury Dri. EH12 —3C **12**
Maybury Rd. EH12 & EH4
    —5C **12**
Maybury Roundabout. EH12
    —5B **12**
May Ct. EH4 —5D **6**
Mayfield Av. EH21 —5D **18**
Mayfield Ct. EH20 —6F **31**
Mayfield Cres. EH20 —6F **31**
Mayfield Cres. EH21 —4C **18**
Mayfield Gdns. EH9 —7K **15**
Mayfield Gdns. La. EH9
    —7K **15**
Mayfield Ind. Est. EH22
(in two parts) —7H **33**
Mayfield Pl. EH21 —5D **18**
Mayfield Pl. EH12 —5F **13**
Mayfield Pl. EH18 —5D **18**
Mayfield Pl. EH22 —7J **33**
Mayfield Rd. EH9 —7K **15**

Mayfield Rd. EH22 —5J **33**
Mayfield Ter. EH9 —7K **15**
Mayshade Pk. EH22 —5C **32**
Mayshade Pk. Cotts. EH22
    —4C **32**
Mayshade Rd. EH22 —4E **30**
Mayville Gdns. EH5 —4B **8**
Mayville Gdns. E. EH5 —4B **8**
Meadowbank. EH8 —2B **16**
Meadowbank Av. EH8 —2B **16**
Meadowbank Cres. EH8
    —2B **16**
Meadowbank Pl. EH8 —2C **16**
Meadowbank Ter. EH8
    —2B **16**
Meadowfield Av. EH8 —4D **16**
Meadowfield Ct. EH8 —4D **16**
Meadowfield Dri. EH8 —4D **16**
Meadowfield Gdns. EH8
    —5D **16**
Meadowfield Rd. EH12
    —3A **12**
Meadowfield Ter. EH8 —5D **16**
Meadowhouse Ct. EH12
    —5G **13**
Meadowhouse Rd. EH12
    —5G **13**
Meadow La. EH8
    —5H **15** (7F **3**)
Meadowmill Cotts. EH33
    —3G **21**
Meadow Pl. EH9 —5G **15**
Meadow Pl. EH25 —7B **30**
*Meadow Pl. La. EH9 —6H **15***
(off Roseneath Ter.)
Meadow Pl. Rd. EH12 —5E **12**
Meadow Rd. EH14 —5B **22**
Meadowside. EH33 —7J **21**
Meadowspot. EH10 —2C **24**
Mearenside. EH12 —3C **12**
Medwin Ho. EH11 —3E **22**
Meeting Ho. Dri. EH33
    —6G **21**
Meggat Pl. EH26 —4C **34**
Meggetland Ter. EH14 —1C **24**
Melgund Ter. EH7 —1H **15**
Melville Cres. EH3 —3E **14**
Melville Dri. EH3 & EH9
    —5G **15**
Melville Dykes Rd. EH18 &
Melville Ga. Rd. EH22 —2C **32**
Melville Grange Cotts. EH18
    —1A **32**
Melville Mains Cotts. EH18
    —2K **31**
Melville Rd. EH22 —3D **32**
Melville St. EH3 —3E **14**
Melville St. La. EH3 —3E **14**
Melville St. La. EH15 —3H **17**
Melville Ter. EH9 —6H **15**
Melville Ter. EH22 —4D **32**
Melville View. EH18 —5K **31**
Mentone Av. EH15 —2H **17**
Mentone Gdns. EH9 —7K **15**
Mentone Ter. EH9 —1K **25**
Merchant St. EH1 —1E **2**
Merchiston Av. EH10 —6E **14**
Merchiston Bank Av. EH10
    —7E **14**
Merchiston Bank Gdns. EH10
    —7E **14**
Merchiston Cres. EH10
    —7E **14**
Merchiston Gdns. EH10
    —1D **24**
Merchiston Gro. EH11 —7C **14**
Merchiston M. EH10 —6E **14**
Merchiston Pk. EH10 —6E **14**
Merchiston Pl. EH10 —6E **14**
Merlyon Way. EH26 —4A **34**
Mertoun Pl. EH11 —6D **14**
Methven Ter. EH18 —7J **31**
Meuse La. EH2 —3H **15** (3E **2**)
Middlebank. EH14 —4E **22**
Middleby St. EH9 —7K **15**
Middlefield. EH7 —7D **8**
Middle Gillsland Rd. EH10
    —7D **14**
Middle Meadow. EH3 —5H **15**

Middle Pier. EH5 —3J **7**
Middleshot. EH14 —4E **22**
Middleshot Sq. EH32 —2F **21**
Mid Liberton. EH16 —2A **26**
Mid Midmar Av. EH10 —2G **25**
Midmar Dri. EH10 —3G **25**
Midmar Gdns. EH10 —2F **25**
Mid New Cultins. EH11
    —2D **22**
Mldpark. EHG —6C **8**
Mid Rd. (Prestonpans) Ind.
    Est. EH32 —4D **20**
Mid Steil. EH10 —3C **24**
Mid Ter. EH30 —5C **4**
Millar Cres. EH10 —1E **24**
Millar Pl. EH10 —1E **24**
Millar Pl. La. EH10 —1E **24**
Millar Rd. EH33 —7G **21**
*Millbrae Wynd. EH14 —2K **23***
(off Inglis Grn. Rd.)
Millerfield Pl. EH9 —6H **15**
Millerhill Rd. EH22 —2H **27**
Miller Row. EH4 —3E **14**
*Miller's Clo. EH22 —2F **33***
(off High St. Dalkeith)
Millhill. EH21 —2F **19**
Millhill Cotts. EH22 —6F **33**
Millhill La. EH21 —2F **19**
Mill La. EH6 —5E **8**
Millstone Brow Cotts. EH23
    —7K **35**
Mill Wynd. EH32 —2D **20**
Milnacre. EH6 —5C **8**
Milne's Ct. EH1 —4D **2**
Milrig Cotts. EH29 —3A **10**
Milton Cres. EH15 —5G **17**
Milton Dri. EH15 —4K **17**
Milton Gdns. N. EH15 —5G **17**
Milton Gdns. S. EH15 —5G **17**
Milton Gro. EH15 —1A **18**
Milton Link. EH15 —5J **17**
Milton Rd. EH15 —5G **17**
Milton Rd. E. EH15 —5J **17**
Milton Rd. W. EH15 —4E **16**
Milton St. EH8 —2A **16**
Milton Ter. EH15 —1A **18**
Miner's Ter. EH21 —7A **20**
Minstrel Ct. EH25 —1B **34**
Minto St. EH9 —6K **15**
Mitchell St. EH6 —5F **9**
Mitchell St. EH22 —2E **32**
Moat Dri. EH14 —7B **14**
Moat Ho. EH14 —7B **14**
Moat Pl. EH14 —7B **14**
Moat St. EH14 —7B **14**
Moat Ter. EH14 —7B **14**
Moat View. EH25 —1A **34**
Moffat Av. EH19 —7H **32**
Moira Pk. EH7 —2E **16**
Moira Ter. EH7 —2E **16**
Moir Av. EH21 —2J **19**
Moir Cres. EH21 —2J **19**
Moir Dri. EH21 —2K **19**
Moir Pl. EH21 —2J **19**
Moir Ter. EH21 —2J **19**
Moncrieffe Ho. EH17 —4D **26**
Moncrieff Ter. EH9 —6J **15**
Monkbarns Gdns. EH16
    —4B **26**
Monksrig Rd. EH26 —7A **34**
Monkswood Rd. EH22
    —2G **35**
Monktonhall Pl. EH21
    —5D **18**
Monktonhall Ter. EH21
    —4D **18**
Monkwood Ct. EH9 —7H **15**
Monmouth Ter. EH3 —5A **8**
Montague St. EH8 —5J **15**
Montagu Ter. EH3 —6A **8**
Monteith Houses. EH23
    —6K **35**
Montgomery St. EH7 —1J **15**
Montgomery St. La. EH7
    —1J **15**
Montpelier. EH10 —6E **14**
Montpelier Pk. EH10 —6E **14**
Montpelier Ter. EH10 —6E **14**
Montrose Ter. EH7
    —2K **15** (1K **3**)

Moorefield Cotts. EH22
    —4J **27**
Moorfoot Ct. EH19 —6A **32**
Moorfoot Pl. EH19 —7A **32**
Moorfoot Pl. EH26 —5B **34**
Moorfoot View. EH19 —7A **32**
Moorfoot View. EH25 —7B **30**
Moray Pl. EH3 —2F **15** (2A **2**)
Moredun Dykes Rd. EH17
    —6D **26**
Moredun Ho. EH4 —7J **7**
Moredun Ho. EH17 —4D **26**
Moredun Pk. Ct. EH17 —5D **26**
Moredun Pk. Dri. EH17
    —5D **26**
Moredun Pk. Gdns. EH17
    —4D **26**
Moredun Pk. Grn. EH17
    —5E **26**
Moredun Pk. Gro. EH17
    —5E **26**
Moredun Pk. Loan. EH17
    —5D **26**
Moredun Pk. Rd. EH17
    —5D **26**
Moredun Pk. St. EH17 —5D **26**
Moredun Pk. View. EH17
    —5E **26**
Moredun Pk. Wlk. EH17
    —5E **26**
Moredun Pk. Way. EH17
    —5D **26**
Moredun Pl. EH17
    —4D **26**
Moredunvale Bank. EH17
    —4D **26**
Moredunvale Grn. EH17
    —4D **26**
Moredunvale Gro. EH17
    —4D **26**
Moredunvale Loan. EH17
    —4D **26**
Moredunvale Pk. EH17
    —4D **26**
Moredunvale Pl. EH17
    —4D **26**
Moredunvale Rd. EH17
    —4C **26**
Moredunvale View. EH17
    —4D **26**
Moredunvale Way. EH17
    —4D **26**
Morison Gdns. EH30 —5B **4**
Morningside Ct. EH10 —2E **24**
Morningside Dri. EH10
    —2D **24**
Morningside Gdns. EH10
    —2D **24**
Morningside Gro. EH10
    —2D **24**
Morningside Pk. EH10
    —1E **24**
Morningside Pl. EH10 —1E **24**
Morningside Rd. EH10
    —7E **14**
Morningside Ter. EH10
    —1E **24**
Morrison Av. EH33 —7J **21**
Morrison Cres. EH3 —4E **14**
Morrison Link. EH3 —4E **14**
Morrison's Clo. EH1 —4G **3**
Morrison's Haven. EH32
    —4A **20**
Morrison St. EH3 —4E **14**
Morris Rd. EH22 —7H **33**
Mortonhall Ga. EH16 —7J **25**
Mortonhall Pk. Av. EH17
    —7K **25**
Mortonhall Pk. Bank. EH17
    —7A **26**
Mortonhall Pk. Cres. EH17
    —7A **26**
Mortonhall Pk. Dri. EH17
    —7A **26**
Mortonhall Pk. Gdns. EH17
    —7K **25**
Mortonhall Pk. Grn. EH17
    —7A **26**
Mortonhall Pk. Gro. EH17
    —7K **25**
Mortonhall Pk. Loan. EH17
    —7K **25**

Mortonhall Pk. Pl. EH17
    —7A **26**
Mortonhall Pk. Ter. EH17
    —7A **26**
Mortonhall Pk. View. EH17
    —7K **25**
Mortonhall Pk. Way. EH17
    —7K **25**
Mortonhall Rd. EH9 —1G **25**
Morton Mains Cotts. EH10
    —1A **30**
Morton St. EH15 —4J **17**
(in two parts)
Morton St. S. EH15 —4J **17**
Morven St. EH4 —2E **12**
Mossend Cotts. EH23 —6K **35**
Mossgiel Wlk. EH16 —3A **26**
Moston Ter. EH9 —7K **15**
Moubray Gro. EH30 —6C **4**
Mound Pl. EH1
    —3G **15** (4D **2**)
Mound, The. EH2
    —3G **15** (3D **2**)
Mountcastle Bank. EH8
    —3F **17**
Mountcastle Cres. EH8
    —3E **16**
Mountcastle Dri. N. EH8 &
    EH15 —3E **16**
Mountcastle Dri. S. EH15
    —4F **17**
Mountcastle Gdns. EH8
    —3E **16**
Mountcastle Grn. EH8 —2E **16**
Mountcastle Gro. EH8 —3E **16**
Mountcastle Loan. EH8
    —3E **16**
Mountcastle Pk. EH8 —2E **16**
Mountcastle Pl. EH8 —2E **16**
Mountcastle Ter. EH8 —3E **16**
Mt. Grange. EH9 —7G **15**
Mounthooly Loan. EH10
    —7G **25**
Mountjoy Ter. EH21 —1H **19**
Mt. Lodge Pl. EH15 —3H **17**
Mt. Vernon Rd. EH16 —4B **26**
Mucklets Av. EH21 —4C **18**
Mucklets Ct. EH21 —4C **18**
Mucklets Cres. EH21 —4C **18**
Mucklets Dri. EH21 —4C **18**
Mucklets Pl. EH21 —4C **18**
Mucklets Rd. EH21 —5B **18**
Muirdale Ter. EH4 —1K **13**
Muirend Av. EH14 —5G **23**
Muirfield Gdns. EH20 —6F **31**
Muir Hall. EH3 —3E **14**
Muirhead Pl. EH26 —3C **34**
Muirhouse Av. EH4 —6C **6**
Muirhouse Bank. EH4 —6C **6**
Muirhouse Cres. EH4 —5E **6**
Muirhouse Dri. EH4 —5D **6**
Muirhouse Gdns. EH4 —5D **6**
Muirhouse Grn. EH4 —6D **6**
Muirhouse Gro. EH4 —5D **6**
Muirhouse Loan. EH4 —5E **6**
Muirhouse Medway. EH4
    —6D **6**
Muirhouse Parkway. EH4
    —5D **6**
Muirhouse Pl. E. EH4 —6E **6**
Muirhouse Pl. W. EH4 —6E **6**
Muirhouse Ter. EH4 —6D **6**
Muirhouse View. EH4 —6D **6**
Muirhouse Way. EH4 —6E **6**
Muirpark. EH22 —4D **32**
Muirpark Ct. EH33 —7J **21**
Muirpark Dri. EH33 —7J **21**
Muirpark Gdns. EH33 —7J **21**
Muirpark Gro. EH33 —7J **21**
Muirpark Pl. EH33 —7J **21**
Muirpark Rd. EH33 —7J **21**
Muirpark Ter. EH33 —7J **21**
Muirpark Wynd. EH33
    —7J **21**
Muirside. EH10 —7C **24**
Muirside Dri. EH33 —7G **19**
Muir Wood Cres. EH14
    —7D **22**
Muir Wood Dri. EH14 —7D **22**

Muir Wood Gro. EH14 —7D **22**
Muir Wood Pl. EH14 —7D **22**
Muir Wood Rd. EH14 —7C **22**
Mulberry Pl. EH6 —5C **8**
Munro Dri. EH13 —7J **23**
Munro Pl. EH3 —7B **8**
Murano Pl. EH7 —1K **15**
Murderdean Rd. EH22 — 7E **32**
Murdoch Ter. EH11 —5E **14**
Murieston Cres. EH11 —5C **14**
Murieston Cres. La. EH11
　　　　　　　—5C **14**
Murieston La. EH11 —6C **14**
Murieston Pl. EH11 —5C **14**
Murieston Rd. EH11 —5C **14**
Murieston Ter. EH11 —5C **14**
Murrayburn App. EH14
　　　　　　　—3F **23**
Murrayburn Dri. EH14 —3E **22**
Murrayburn Gdns. EH14
　　　　　　　—3G **23**
Murrayburn Ga. EH14 —4F **23**
Murrayburn Grn. EH14
　　　　　　　—3G **23**
Murrayburn Gro. EH14
　　　　　　　—3G **23**
Murrayburn Pk. EH14 —3F **23**
Murrayburn Pl. EH14 —3F **23**
Murrayburn Rd. EH14 —3F **23**
Murray Cotts. EH12 —5E **12**
Murrayfield Av. EH12 —4B **14**
Murrayfield Dri. EH12 —4A **14**
Murrayfield Gdns. EH12
　　　　　　　—4B **14**
Murrayfield Pl. EH12 —4B **14**
Murrayfield Rd. EH12 —3A **14**
Murray Pl. EH12 —5G **13**
Murrays Brae, The. EH17
　　　　　　　—1F **31**
Murrays, The. EH17 —1F **31**
Musselburgh By-Pass. EH15 &
　　　　　EH21 —6J **17**
Musselburgh Rd. EH15
　　　　　　　—4K **17**
Musselburgh Rd. EH22
　　　　　　　—1F **33**
Myre Dale. EH19 —7B **32**
Myreside Ct. EH10 —2D **24**
Myreside Rd. EH10 —1D **24**
Myrtle Cres. EH25 —7B **30**
Myrtle Gro. EH22 —6J **33**
Myrtle Ter. EH11 —6C **14**

Namur Rd. EH26 —3C **34**
Nantwich Dri. EH7 —7K **9**
Napier Rd. EH10 —7D **14**
Neidpath Ct. EH12 —4C **12**
(off Craigievar Wynd)
Nellfield. EH16 —4B **26**
Nelson Pl. EH3 —1G **15** (1D **2**)
Nelson St. EH3 —2G **15** (1D **2**)
Netherby Rd. EH5 —5K **7**
Nether Craigour. EH17
　　　　　　　—3D **26**
Nether Craigwell. EH8 —3J **3**
Nether Currie Cres. EH14
　　　　　　　—7D **22**
Nether Currie Pl. EH14
　　　　　　　—7D **22**
Nether Currie Rd. EH14
　　　　　　　—7D **22**
Nethershot Rd. EH32 —2E **20**
Nevis Gdns. EH26 —5D **34**
New Arthur Pl. EH8
　　　　　　—4J **15** (5H **3**)
Newbattle Abbey Cres. EH22
　　　　　　　—6E **32**
Newbattle Ind. Est. EH22
(in two parts)　　—7H **33**
Newbattle Rd. EH22 —3E **32**
Newbattle Ter. EH10 —7F **15**
New Belfield. EH8 —4E **16**
New Bells Ct. EH6 —5F **9**
Newbigging. EH21 —2F **19**
(in two parts)
Newbridge Ind. Est. EH28
　　　　　　　—6B **10**
New Broompark. EH5 —3H **7**
New Broughton. EH3 —1H **15**

Newbyres Av. EH23 —5H **35**
Newbyres Cres. EH23 —6H **35**
Newcraighall Dri. EH21
　　　　　　　—7K **17**
Newcraighall Rd. EH15 & EH21
　　　　　　　—7H **17**
Newhailes Av. EH21 —2C **18**
Newhailes Cres. EH21 —2B **18**
Newhailes Ind. Est. EH21
　　　　　　　—3B **18**
Newhailes Rd. EH21 —3B **18**
Newhalls Rd. EH30 —5D **4**
Newhaven Pl. EH6 —3C **8**
Newhaven Rd. EH6 —4C **8**
New Hunterfield. EH23
　　　　　　　—4G **35**
Newington Rd. EH9 —6J **15**
New John's Pl. EH8
　　　　　　—5J **15** (7H **3**)
Newkirkgate. EH6 —5E **8**
(off Kirkgate)
Newkirkgate Shoppping Cen.
(off Kirkgate)　EH6 —5E **8**
New Lairdship Yards. EH11
　　　　　　　—1F **23**
Newlands Pk. EH9 —7K **15**
New La. EH6 —4C **8**
New Liston Rd. EH29 —3A **10**
Newmains Farm La. EH29
　　　　　　　—1A **10**
Newmains Rd. EH29 —1A **10**
New Market Rd. EH14 —1A **24**
New Mart Rd. EH14 —1K **23**
New Meadowspott. EH22
　　　　　　　—3E **32**
Newmills Av. EH14 —1F **29**
Newmills Ct. EH14 —2F **29**
Newmills Cres. EH14 —2F **29**
Newmills Gro. EH14 —2F **29**
Newmills Rd. EH14 —1E **28**
Newmills Rd. EH22 —2F **33**
New Orchardfield. EH6 —6E **8**
Newport St. EH3
　　　　　　—4F **15** (6A **2**)
New Row. EH33 —6G **21**
New St Andrew's Ho. EH1
　　　　　　　—2F **3**
New Skinner's Clo. EH1
　　　　　　　—4G **3**
New St. EH8 —3J **15** (3G **3**)
New St. EH17 —7D **26**
New St. EH21 —2C **18**
New St. EH32 —1A **20**
(Cockenzie)
New St. EH32 —3D **20**
(Prestonpans)
New St. EH33 —5G **21**
New Swanston. EH10 —7D **24**
Newton Chu. Rd. EH22
　　　　　　　—5H **27**
Newton St. EH11 —6C **14**
Newton St. EH22 —5H **33**
Newton Village. EH22 —4K **27**
New Tower Pl. EH15 —2H **17**
Nicolson Sq. EH8
　　　　　　—4J **15** (6G **3**)
Nicolson St. EH8
　　　　　　—4J **15** (5G **3**)
Niddrie Cotts. EH15 —7J **17**
Niddrie Farm Gro. EH16
　　　　　　　—7E **16**
Niddrie Ho. Av. EH16 —1F **27**
Niddrie Ho. Dri. EH16
　　　　　　　—7G **17**
Niddrie Ho. Gdns. EH16
　　　　　　　—1F **27**
Niddrie Ho. Gro. EH16 —1F **27**
Niddrie Ho. Pk. EH16 —1F **27**
Niddrie Ho. Sq. EH16 —1G **27**
Niddrie Mains Ct. EH16
　　　　　　　—7G **17**
Niddrie Mains Dri. EH16
　　　　　　　—7E **16**
Niddrie Mains Rd. EH16 &
　　　　　EH15 —7D **16**
Niddrie Mains Ter. EH16
　　　　　　　—7E **16**
Niddrie Marischal Cres. EH16
　　　　　　　—7F **17**

Niddrie Marischal Dri. EH16
　　　　　　　—1F **27**
Niddrie Marischal Gdns. EH16
　　　　　　　—7F **17**
Niddrie Marischal Grn. EH16
　　　　　　　—1F **27**
Niddrie Marischal Gro. EH16
　　　　　　　—7G **17**
Niddrie Marischal Loan EH16
　　　　　　　—7F **17**
Niddrie Marischal Pl. EH16
　　　　　　　—7F **17**
Niddrie Marischal Rd. EH16
　　　　　　　—7G **17**
Niddrie Marischal St. EH16
　　　　　　　—7F **17**
Niddrie Mill Av. EH15 —7G **17**
Niddrie Mill Cres. EH15
　　　　　　　—7G **17**
Niddrie Mill Dri. EH15 —7G **17**
Niddrie Mill Gro. EH15
　　　　　　　—7G **17**
Niddrie Mill Pl. EH15 —7G **17**
Niddrie Mill Ter. EH15 —7G **17**
Niddry St. EH1 —3J **15** (4F **3**)
Niddry St. S. EH1
　　　　　　—4J **15** (5G **3**)
Nigel Loan. EH16 —4B **26**
Nile Gro. EH10 —1F **25**
Nimmo Av. EH32 —3E **20**
Ninth St. EH22 —7G **33**
Nisbet Ct. EH7 —7G **9**
Nivenskowe Caravan Pk.
　　　　　EH20 —6B **30**
Niven's Knowe Rd. EH20
　　　　　　　—6C **30**
Nobel Pl. EH25 —1A **34**
Noble Pl. EH6 —6G **9**
N. Bank Rd. EH32 —3C **20**
N. Bank St. EH1
　　　　　　—3H **15** (4E **2**)
North Bri. EH1 —3H **15** (3F **3**)
North Bri. Arc. EH1 —4F **3**
N. Bughtlin Bank. EH12
　　　　　　　—2D **12**
N. Bughtlin Brae. EH12
　　　　　　　—2D **12**
N. Bughtlinfield. EH12 —2C **12**
N. Bughtlin Ga. EH12 —2D **12**
N. Bughtlin Pl. EH12 —2D **12**
N. Bughtlinrig. EH12 —2C **12**
N. Bughtlin Rd. EH12 —2D **12**
N. Bughtlinside. EH12 —2C **12**
N. Bughtlin Wlk. EH12 —2D **12**
N. Cairntow. EH16 —6D **16**
N. Castle St. EH2
　　　　　　—2F **15** (2B **2**)
N. Charlotte St. EH2
　　　　　　—3F **15** (2A **2**)
N. Clyde St. La. EH1
　　　　　　—2H **15** (1E **2**)
Northcote St. EH11 —5D **14**
North Cres. EH32 —3E **20**
N. E. Circus Pl. EH3
　　　　　　—2F **15** (1B **2**)
N. E. Thistle St. La. EH2
　　　　　　　—2D **2**
N. Fort St. EH6 —4D **8**
N. Grange Av. EH32 —4C **20**
N. Grange Gro. EH32 —3D **20**
N. Grange Rd. EH32 —3D **20**
N. Gray's Clo. EH1 —4F **3**
N. Greens. EH15 —6H **17**
N. Gyle Av. EH12 —5D **12**
N. Gyle Dri. EH12 —4D **12**
N. Gyle Farm Cl. EH12
　　　　　　　—5C **12**
N. Gyle Farm La. EH12
　　　　　　　—5C **12**
N. Gyle Gro. EH12 —4C **12**
N. Gyle Loan. EH12 —4C **12**
N. Gyle Pk. EH12 —4C **12**
N. Gyle Rd. EH12 —4D **12**
N. Gyle Ter. EH12 —5C **12**
N. High St. EH21 —2D **18**
(in three parts)
N. Hillhousefield. EH6 —4D **8**
N. Junction St. EH6 —4D **8**
Northlawn Ct. EH4 —6B **6**
Northlawn Ter. EH4 —6B **6**
N. Leith Mill. EH6 —4E **8**
N. Leith Sands. EH6 —4E **8**
N. Lorimer Pl. EH32 —1A **20**
N. Meadow Wlk. EH3 & EH8
　　　　　　—5G **15** (7C **2**)
N. Meggetland. EH14 —1C **24**
Northpark. EH6 —5C **8**
North Pk. Ter. EH4 —1E **14**
N. Peffer Pl. EH16 —7D **16**
N. Richmond St. EH8
　　　　　　—4J **15** (5G **3**)
N. St Andrew La. EH2
　　　　　　—2H **15** (2E **2**)
N. St Andrew St. EH2
　　　　　　—2H **15** (1E **2**)
N. St David St. EH2
　　　　　　—2H **15** (2D **2**)
N. Seton Pk. EH32 —1B **20**
North St. EH28 —7B **10**
Northumberland Pl. EH3
　　　　　　　—1D **2**
Northumberland Pl. La. EH3
　　　　　　　—1D **2**
Northumberland St. EH3
　　　　　　—2G **15** (1C **2**)
Northumberland St. N. E. La.
　　　EH3 —2G **15** (1D **2**)
Northumberland St. N. W. La.
　　　EH3 —2G **15** (1D **2**)
Northumberland St. S. E. La.
　　　EH3 —2G **15** (1D **2**)
Northumberland St. S. W. La.
　　　EH3 —2G **15** (1D **2**)
Northview Ct. EH4 —5E **6**
North Wlk., The. EH10
　　　　　　　—2E **24**
N. Way, The. EH8 —3D **16**
N. Werber Pk. EH4 —6H **7**
N. W. Circus Pl. EH3
　　　　　　—2F **15** (1A **2**)
N. W. Thistle St. La. EH2
　　　　　　　—2D **2**
N. Wynd. EH22 —2F **33**
Norton Mains Cotts. EH28
　　　　　　　—6F **11**
Norton Pk. EH7 —1A **16**

Old Assembly Clo. EH1 —4F **3**
Old Broughton. EH3 —1H **15**
Old Burdiehouse Rd. EH17
　　　　　　　—2D **30**

Old Chu. La. EH15 —5C **16**
Old Craighall Junction. EH21
　　　　　　　—6D **18**
Old Craighall Rd. EH22 & EH21
　　　　　　　—5K **27**
Old Dalkeith Rd. EH16 & EH22
　　　　　　　—1B **26**
Old Dalkeith Rd. EH17
　　　　　　　—4F **27**
Old Dalkeith Rd. EH17
　　　　　　　—1C **32**
Old Edinburgh Rd. EH22
　　　　　　　—2E **32**
Old Farm Av. EH13 —5K **23**
Old Farm Pl. EH13 —6K **23**
Old Fishmarket Clo. EH1
　　　　　—3H **15** (4F **3**)
Old Kirk Rd. EH12 —4G **13**
Old Liston Rd. EH28 —5A **10**
Old Mill La. EH16 —2A **26**
Old Newmills Rd. EH14
　　　　　　　—2F **29**
Old Pentland Rd. EH10
　　　　　　　—5A **30**
Old Playhouse Clo. EH8
　　　　　　　—4H **3**
Old Star Bank. EH22 —7E **32**
Old Tolbooth Wynd. EH8
　　　　　　—3J **15** (3H **3**)
Olivebank Rd. EH21 —2C **18**
Orchard Bank. EH4 —2C **14**
Orchard Brae. EH4 —1D **14**
Orchard Brae Av. EH4 —2C **14**
Orchard Brae Gdns. EH4
　　　　　　　—2C **14**
Orchard Brae. Gdns. W. EH4
　　　　　　　—2C **14**
Orchard Brae W. EH4 —1D **14**
Orchard Cres. EH4 —2B **14**
Orchard Cres. EH32 —3D **20**
Orchard Dri. EH4 —2B **14**
Orchardfield Av. EH12 —5F **13**
Orchardfield La. EH6 —7E **8**
Orchard Gro. EH4 —2D **14**
Orchardhead Loan. EH16
　　　　　　　—4A **26**
Orchardhead Rd. EH16
　　　　　　　—3A **26**
Orchard Pl. EH4 —1C **14**
Orchard Rd. EH4 —2C **14**
Orchard Rd. S. EH4 —2B **14**
Orchard Ter. EH4 —2C **14**
Orchard, The. EH33 —5G **21**
Orchard Toll. EH4 —2C **14**
Orchard View. EH22 —3D **32**
Origo Cen. EH14 —3B **22**
Ormelie Ter. EH15 —3J **17**
Ormidale Ter. EH12 —4A **14**
Ormiston Cres. E. EH33
　　　　　　　—6J **21**
Ormiston Cres. W. EH33
　　　　　　　—6J **21**
Ormiston Pl. EH32 —3C **20**
Ormiston Rd. EH33 —6H **21**
Ormiston Ter. EH12 —5F **13**
Orrok Pk. EH16 —2A **26**
Orwell Pl. EH11 —5D **14**
Orwell Ter. EH11 —5D **14**
Osborne Ct. EH32 —1A **20**
Osborne Ter. EH12 —4D **14**
Osborne Ter. EH32 —1A **20**
Oswald Ct. EH9 —1H **25**
Oswald Rd. EH9 —1H **25**
Oswald Ter. EH12 —5F **13**
Oswald Ter. EH32 —3E **20**
Otterburn Pk. EH14 —4K **23**
Oxcars Ct. EH4 —5D **6**
Oxcraig St. EH5 —3J **7**
Oxford St. EH8 —5K **15**
Oxford Ter. EH4 —2E **14**
Oxgangs Av. EH13 —6C **24**
Oxgangs Bank. EH13 —6D **24**
Oxgangs Brae. EH13 —6D **24**
Oxgangs B'way. EH13 —6D **24**
(off Oxgangs Bank)
Oxgangs Cres. EH13 —5D **24**
Oxgangs Dri. EH13 —5C **24**
Oxgangs Farm Av. EH13
　　　　　　　—6C **24**

Oxgangs Farm Dri. EH13
—6C **24**
Oxgangs Farm Gdns. EH13
—6C **24**
Oxgangs Farm Gro. EH13
—6C **24**
Oxgangs Farm Loan. EH13
—6C **24**
Oxgangs Farm Ter. EH13
—6C **24**
Oxgangs Gdns. EH13 —5C **24**
Oxgangs Grn. EH13 —5D **24**
Oxgangs Gro. EH13 —5D **24**
Oxgangs Hill. EH13 —5D **24**
Oxgangs Ho. EH13 —5D **24**
Oxgangs Loan. EH13 —5D **24**
Oxgangs Medway. EH13
—6D **24**
Oxgangs Pk. EH13 —5D **24**
Oxgangs Path. EH13 —6D **24**
Oxgangs Path E. EH13
(off Oxgangs Brae) —6D **24**
Oxgangs Pl. EH13 —5C **24**
Oxgangs Rise. EH13 —5D **24**
Oxgangs Rd. EH13 & EH10
—7D **24**
Oxgangs Rd. N. EH14 & EH13
—4B **24**
Oxgangs Row. EH13 —6D **24**
Oxgangs Ter. EH13 —6C **24**
Oxgangs View. EH13 —5D **24**
Ox Wlk. EH32 —3C **20**

Paddockholm, The. EH12
—5G **13**
Paddock, The. EH21 —1F **19**
Paisley Av. EH8 —3D **16**
Paisley Clo. EH1 —4G **3**
Paisley Cres. EH8 —3C **16**
Paisley Dri. EH8 —4D **16**
Paisley Gdns. EH8 —3C **16**
Paisley Gro. EH8 —4D **16**
Paisley Ter. EH8 —3C **16**
Pallas St. EH5 —2H **7**
Palmer Pl. EH14 —1H **29**
Palmer Rd. EH14 —7B **22**
Palmerston Pl. EH12 —3D **14**
Palmerston Pl. La. EH12
—4E **14**
Palmerston Rd. EH9 —6H **15**
Pandore Wlk. EH32 —3C **20**
Pankhurst Loan. EH22
—2J **33**
Panmure Clo. EH8 —3H **3**
Panmure Pl. EH3
—5G **15** (7C **2**)
Pape's Cotts. EH12 —4E **12**
Paradykes Av. EH20 —5D **30**
Park Av. EH15 —4G **17**
Park Av. EH20 —6D **30**
Park Av. EH21 —3G **19**
Park Av. EH23 —5H **35**
Park Av. EH25 —7A **30**
Park Ct. EH7 —2E **16**
Park Cres. EH16 —4B **26**
Park Cres. EH19 —6A **32**
Park Cres. EH20 —6E **30**
Park Cres. EH22 —5H **33**
Parker Av. EH7 —2E **16**
Parker Rd. EH7 —2E **16**
Parker Ter. EH7 —2F **17**
Park Gdns. EH16 —4B **26**
Park Gro. EH16 —5B **26**
Parkgrove Av. EH4 —1E **12**
Parkgrove Bank. EH4 —1E **12**
Parkgrove Cres. EH4 —1E **12**
Parkgrove Dri. EH4 —1D **12**
Parkgrove Gdns. EH4 —1E **12**
Parkgrove Grn. EH4 —1E **12**
Parkgrove Loan. EH4 —1E **12**
Parkgrove Neuk. EH4 —1E **12**
Parkgrove Path. EH4 —1F **13**
Parkgrove Pl. EH4 —1E **12**
Park Gro. Pl. EH21 —3G **19**
Parkgrove Rd. EH4 —1E **12**
Parkgrove Row. EH4 —1E **12**
Parkgrove St. EH4 —1F **13**
Parkgrove Ter. EH4 —1E **12**

Park Gro. Ter. EH21 —3G **19**
Parkgrove View. EH4 —1E **12**
Parkhead Av. EH11 —2G **23**
Parkhead Cres. EH11 —2G **23**
Parkhead Dri. EH11 —2G **23**
Parkhead Gdns. EH11
—2G **23**
Parkhead Gro. EH11 —2G **23**
Parkhead Loan. EH11 —2H **24**
Parkhead Pk. EH22 —5H **33**
Parkhead Pl. EH11 —2G **23**
Parkhead Pl. EH22 —5H **33**
Parkhead St. EH11 —2G **23**
Parkhead Ter. EH11 —2H **23**
Parkhead View. EH11
—2G **23**
Parkhill. EH23 —5G **35**
Park La. EH15 —4G **17**
Park La. EH21 —3G **19**
Park Pl. EH6 —4B **8**
Park Rd. EH6 —4B **8**
Park Rd. EH19 —6A **32**
Park Rd. EH22 —3E **32**
(Dalkeith)
Park Rd. EH22 —7G **33**
(Newtongrange)
Park Rd. EH23 —5H **35**
Park Rd. EH32 —1B **20**
Parkside. EH28 —5A **10**
Parkside Pl. EH22 —2F **33**
Parkside St. EH8 —5K **15**
Parkside Ter. EH16 —5K **15**
Park Ter. EH21 —4A **18**
Parkvale Pl. EH6 —6G **9**
Park View. EH20 —6E **30**
Park View. EH21 —3G **19**
(Musselburgh)
Park View. EH21 —7K **17**
(Newcraighall)
Park View. EH32 —3F **21**
Park View E. EH32 —1B **20**
Park View W. EH32 —1B **20**
Parliament Sq. EH1 —4E **2**
Parliament St. EH6 —5E **8**
Parrotshot. EH15 —6H **17**
Parsonage. EH21 —2F **19**
Parsons Grn. Ter. EH8 —2C **16**
Parson's Pool. EH19 —7B **32**
Path Brae. EH29 —2A **10**
Patie's Rd. EH14 —4A **24**
Patrick St. EH8 —7G **3**
Patriot Hall. EH3 —1F **15**
Pattison St. EH6 —5F **9**
Paulsfield. EH6 —6C **8**
Peacock Ct. EH6 —4C **8**
Peacock Ride. EH30 —1D **4**
Peacocktail Clo. EH15 —7H **17**
Pearce Av. EH12 —4E **12**
Pearce Gro. EH12 —4E **12**
Pearce Rd. EH12 —4E **12**
Peatville Gdns. EH14 —3J **23**
Peatville Ter. EH14 —3J **23**
Pedrixknowe. EH14 —1B **24**
Peebles Rd. EH26 —7C **34**
Peel Ter. EH9 —7K **15**
Peffer Bank. EH16 —7D **16**
Peffermill Ct. EH16 —1C **26**
Peffermill Rd. EH16 —1B **26**
Peffer Pl. EH16 —7D **16**
Peffer St. EH16 —7D **16**
Peggy's Mill Rd. EH4 —6H **5**
Pembroke Pl. EH12 —4C **14**
Pence St. EH16 —6K **15**
Pendreich Av. EH19 —5B **32**
Pendreich Dri. EH19 —5B **32**
Pendreich Gro. EH19 —5B **32**
Pendreich Ter. EH19 —5B **32**
Pendreich View. EH19
—5B **32**
Pend, The. EH30 —6A **4**
Penicuik Rd. EH25 —1A **34**
Pennywell Cotts. EH4 —4E **6**
Pennywell Gdns. EH4 —5D **6**
Pennywell Gro. EH4 —5E **6**
Pennywell Medway. EH4
—5D **6**
Pennywell Pl. EH4 —5E **6**
Pennywell Rd. EH4 —5E **6**
Pennywell Vs. EH4 —4E **6**

Pentland Av. EH13 —6J **23**
Pentland Av. EH14 —1H **29**
Pentland Av. EH23 —3G **35**
Pentland Av. EH26 —5B **34**
Pentland Caravan Pk. EH20
—5B **30**
Pentland Cres. EH10 —5E **24**
Pentland Cres. EH24 —6F **35**
Pentland Dri. EH10 —6D **24**
Pentland Gdns. EH10 —5E **24**
Pentland Gro. EH10 —5E **24**
Pentland Ind. Est. EH20
—6C **30**
Pentland Pl. EH14 —1H **29**
Pentland Rd. EH10 & EH20
—3A **30**
Pentland Rd. EH13 —5J **23**
Pentland Rd. EH19 —7J **31**
Pentland Ter. EH10 —4E **24**
(in two parts)
Pentland Ter. EH26 —5B **34**
Pentland View. EH10 —6E **24**
Pentland View. EH14 —1H **29**
Pentland View. EH22 —3H **33**
Pentland View Ct. EH14
—1J **29**
Pentland View Cres. EH25
—1A **34**
Pentland View Pl. EH25
—1A **34**
Pentland View Rd EH25
—1A **34**
Pentland View Rd. EH29
—2A **10**
Pentland View Ter. EH25
—1A **34**
Pentland Vs. EH14 —7E **22**
Persevere Ct. EH6 —4E **8**
(off Admiralty St.)
Perth St. EH3 —1F **15**
Pettigrew's Clo. EH22 —2F **33**
Peveril Ter. EH16 —4A **26**
Philip Pl. EH26 —4B **34**
Picardy Pl. EH1 —2H **15** (1F **3**)
Pier Pl. EH6 —3B **8**
Piersfield Gro. EH8 —2D **16**
Piersfield Pl. EH8 —2D **16**
Piersfield Ter. EH8 —2D **16**
Piershill La. EH8 —2C **16**
Piershill Pl. EH8 —2C **16**
Piershill Sq. E. EH8 —2D **16**
Piershill Sq. W. EH8 —2C **16**
Piershill Ter. EH8 —2D **16**
Pilrig Cotts. EH6 —7E **8**
Pilrig Gdns. EH6 —7D **8**
Pilrig Glebe. EH6 —7E **8**
Pilrig Ho. Clo. EH6 —6D **8**
Pilrig Pl. EH6 —7E **8**
Pilrig St. EH6 —7D **8**
Pilton Av. EH5 —5G **7**
Pilton Cres. EH5 —5J **7**
Pilton Dri. EH5 —5H **7**
Pilton Dri. N. EH5 —4H **7**
Pilton Gdns. EH5 —5H **7**
Pilton Loan. EH5 —5H **7**
Pilton Pk. EH5 —5H **7**
Pilton Pl. EH5 —5H **7**
Pinewood Pl. EH22 —7K **33**
Pinewood Rd. EH22 —7K **33**
Pinewood View. EH22
—7K **33**
Pinkhill. EH12 —5H **13**
Pinkie Av. EH21 —3G **19**
Pinkie Dri. EH21 —3G **19**
Pinkie Hill Cres. EH21
—3G **19**
Pinkie Hill Farm Cotts. EH21
—4G **19**
Pinkie Pl. EH21 —3G **19**
Pinkie Rd. EH21 —3F **19**
Pinkie Ter. EH21 —3G **19**
Pinkie Wlk. EH33 —7G **21**
Pipe La. EH15 —2G **17**
Pipe St. EH15 —2G **17**
Pirniefield Bank. EH6 —6H **9**
Pirniefield Gdns. EH6 —6H **9**
Pirniefield Gro. EH6 —6H **9**
Pirniefield Pl. EH6 —6H **9**
Pirniefield Ter. EH6 —6H **9**
Pirrie St. EH6 —6E **8**

Pitlochry Pl. EH7 —1A **16**
Pitsligo Rd. EH10 —7F **15**
Pittencrief Ct. EH21 —2H **19**
Pitt St. EH6 —5C **8**
Pittville St. EH15 —3H **17**
Pittville St. La. EH15 —3H **17**
Place Charente. EH22 —2H **33**
Playfair Steps. EH2 —4D **2**
Pleasance. EH8 —4J **15** (5H **3**)
Plewlandcroft. EH30 —5B **4**
Plewlands Av. EH10 —2D **24**
Plewlands Gdns. EH10
—2D **24**
Plewlands Pl. EH30 —6B **4**
Plewlands Ter. EH10 —2D **24**
Pleydell Pl. EH16 —4B **26**
Poet's Glen. EH14 —1K **29**
Pollock Halls of Residence.
EH16 —6A **16**
Pollock's Clo. EH1 —5E **2**
Polson Gdns. EH22 —3H **33**
Polton Av. Rd. EH19 —7J **31**
Polton Bank. EH18 —7G **31**
Polton Bank Ter. EH18
—7H **31**
Polton Cotts. EH18 —7G **31**
Polton Ct. EH19 —6A **32**
Polton Dri. EH18 —7J **31**
Polton Gdns. EH18 —6K **31**
Polton Pl. EH19 —6A **32**
Polton Rd. EH18 —6K **31**
(Lasswade)
Polton Rd. EH20 & EH18
—6F **31**
(Loanhead & Polton)
Polton Rd. W. EH18 —7H **31**
Polton St. EH19 —7A **32**
Polton Ter. EH18 —6K **31**
Polwarth Cres. EH11 —6E **14**
Polwarth Cres. EH32 —3E **20**
Polwarth Gdns. EH11 —6D **14**
Polwarth Grn. EH11 —6D **14**
Polwarth Pk. EH11 —6D **14**
Polwarth Pl. EH11 —6D **14**
Polwarth Ter. EH11 —1C **24**
Polwarth Ter. EH32 —3E **20**
Pomathorn Bank. EH26
—7C **34**
Pomathorn Rd. EH26 —7C **34**
Ponton St. EH3 —5F **15** (7B **2**)
Poplar La. EH6 —5G **9**
Poplar Path. EH20 —6B **30**
Poplar St. EH22 —7K **33**
Poplar Ter. EH19 —7A **32**
Porterfield Rd. EH4 —7H **7**
Portgower Pl. EH4 —1E **14**
Portland Pl. EH6 —4D **8**
(off Lindsay Rd.)
Portland St. EH6 —4D **8**
Portland Ter. EH6 —4D **8**
Portobello High St. EH15
—2G **17**
Portobello Rd. EH8 & EH7
—2C **16**
Portsburgh Sq. EH1 —5C **2**
Post Rd. EH33 —5F **21**
Potterrow. EH8 —4H **15** (6F **3**)
Potterrow Port. EH8 —6F **3**
Pottery, The. EH15 —2G **17**
Pottery, The. EH32 —3C **20**
Povert Rd. EH23 —5F **35**
Powderhall Brae. EH23
—7J **35**
Preston Av. EH32 —3F **21**
Preston Ct. EH32 —4D **20**
Preston Cres. EH32 —2F **21**
Preston Cross Cotts. EH32
—3E **20**
Prestonfield Av. EH16
—7A **16**
Prestonfield Bank. EH16
—7A **16**
Prestonfield Cres. EH16
—1A **26**
Prestonfield Gdns. EH16
—7A **16**
Prestonfield Rd. EH16
—7A **16**
Prestonfield Ter. EH16
—7A **16**

Prestongrange Rd. EH32
—3B **20**
Prestongrange Ter. EH32
—3C **20**
Prestonhall Cres. EH24
—6F **35**
Prestonhall Rd. EH24 —7F **35**
Preston Rd. EH32 —4D **20**
Preston St. EH24 —7F **35**
Preston Ter. EH32 —3F **21**
Preston Tower. EH32 —3D **20**
Priestfield Av. EH16 —7B **16**
Priestfield Cres. EH16
—7B **16**
Priestfield Gdns. EH16
—7B **16**
Priestfield Gro. EH16 —6B **16**
Priestfield Rd. EH16 —6A **16**
Priestfield Rd. N. EH16
—6A **16**
Primrose Bank Rd. EH5
—4A **8**
Primrose Cres. EH22 —3H **33**
Primrose Gdns. EH30 —6C **4**
Primrose St. EH6 —6F **9**
Primrose Ter. EH11 —6C **14**
Primrose Ter. EH22 —3H **33**
Prince Regent St. EH6 —4D **8**
Princes St. EH2
—3F **15** (4A **2**)
Priory Gro. EH30 —6B **4**
Private Rd. EH23 —7J **35**
Promenade. EH15 —1F **17**
Promenade. EH21 —1D **18**
Promenade. EH15 —2G **17**
Prospect Bank Cres. EH6
—6H **9**
Prospect Bank Gdns. EH6
—7G **9**
Prospect Bank Gro. EH6
—6H **9**
Prospect Bank Pl. EH6 —6H **9**
Prospect Bank Rd. EH6
—6G **9**
Prospect Bank Ter. EH6
—6H **9**
Provost Milne Gro. EH30
—7C **4**
Pryde Av. EH19 —6K **31**
Pryde Ter. EH19 —6K **31**
Pypers Wynd. EH32 —2D **20**

Quadrant, The. EH26 —5C **34**
Quality St. EH4 —7C **6**
Quality St. La. EH4 —7C **6**
Quarrybank. EH14 —4E **22**
Quarrybank Clo. EH14
—4E **22**
Quarrybank Ct. EH14 —4E **22**
Quarrybank End. EH14
—4E **22**
Quarrybank Rd. EH14 —4E **22**
Quarry Clo. EH8 —7G **3**
Quarry Cotts. EH15 —7H **17**
Quarryfoot Gdns. EH19
—6A **32**
Quarryfoot Grn. EH19 —6A **32**
Quarryfoot Pl. EH19 —6A **32**
Quarry Howe. EH14 —4E **28**
Quarry Rd. EH23 —5J **35**
Quarry View. EH14 —4E **22**
Quayside St. EH6 —5E **8**
Queen Anne Dri. EH28
—6B **10**
Queen Charlotte La. EH6
—5F **9**
Queen Charlotte St. EH6
—5F **9**
Queen Margaret Clo. EH10
—7H **25**
Queen Margaret Dri. EH30
—6C **4**
Queen's Av. EH4 —1K **13**
Queen's Av. S. EH4 —1A **14**
Queen's Bay Cres. EH15
—4K **17**
Queen's Cres. EH9 —7K **15**
Queen's Dri. EH8
—4K **15** (6J **3**)

Queensferry Rd. EH4 —7G 5 (Cramond)
Queensferry Rd. EH4 —2A 14 (Edinburgh)
Queensferry St. EH29 —1A 10
Queensferry St. EH2 —3E 14
Queensferry St. La. EH2 —3F 15 (4A 2)
Queensferry Ter. EH4 —2C 14
Queen's Gdns. EH4 —1A 14
Queen's Pk. Av. EH8 —2B 16
Queen's Pk. EH8 —3C 16
Queen's Pk. Ct. EH8 —3C 16
Queen's Rd. EH4 —1A 14
Queen St. EH2 —2F 15 (2B 2)
Queen St. Gdns. E. EH3 —2G 15 (1D 2)
Queen St. Gdns. W. EH3 —2G 15 (2C 2)
Queen's Wlk. EH16 —7E 16
Queensway. EH26 —4B 34
Quilts, The. EH6 —5E 8
Quilts Wynd. EH6 —5D 8

Radical Rd. EH8 —4K 15
Raeburn M. EH4 —1E 14
Raeburn Pl. EH4 —1E 14
Raeburn St. EH4 —1E 14
Rae's Gdns. EH19 —6A 32
Ramillies Ct. EH26 —3D 34
Ramsay Cres. FH22 —1K 35
Ramsay Garden. EH1 —3G 15 (4D 2)
Ramsay La. EH1 —3G 15 (4D 2)
Ramsay Pl. EH15 —2H 17
Ramsay Ter. EH18 —7J 31
Ramsay Wlk. EH22 —1K 35
Randolph Cir. EH3 —3E 14
Randolph Cliff. EH3 —3E 14
Randolph La. EH3 —3F 15 (3A 2)
Randolph Pl. EH3 —3F 15 (3A 2)
Rankeillor St. EH8 —5J 15 (7H 3)
Ranklin Av. EH9 —2K 25
Rankin Dri. EH9 —2J 25
Rankin Rd. EH9 —1K 25
Rannoch Gro. EH4 —2F 13
Rannoch Pl. EH4 —2F 13
Rannoch Rd. EH4 —2F 13
Rannoch Ter. EH4 —2F 13
Ransome Gdns. EH4 —2F 13
Ratcliffe Ter. EH9 —7J 15
Rathbone Pl. EH15 —2G 17
Ratho Pk. Rd. EH28 —7C 10
Ravelrig Hill. EH14 —3D 28
Ravelrig Pk. EH14 —3D 28
Ravelrig Rd. EH14 —2D 28
Ravelston Ct. EH12 —3B 14 —3A 14
Ravelston Dykes. EH12 & EH4 —3A 14
Ravelston Dykes La. EH4 —3J 13
Ravelston Dykes Rd. EH4 —2K 13
Ravelston Garden. EH4 —3A 14
Ravelston Heights. EH4 —2A 14
Ravelston Ho. Gro. EH4 —2A 14
Ravelston Ho. Loan. EH4 —2A 14
Ravelston Ho. Pk. EH4 —2A 14
Ravelston Ho. Rd. EH4 —2A 14
Ravelston Pk. EH4 —3C 14
Ravelston Pl. EH4 —3D 14
Ravelston Rise. EH4 —3A 14
Ravelston Ter. EH4 —2D 14
Ravelsykes Rd. EH26 —7A 34
Ravendean Gdns. EH26 —7A 34
Ravenscroft Gdns. EH17 —7E 26
Ravenscroft Pl. EH17 —7D 26
Ravenscroft St. EH17 —7E 26

Ravensheugh Cres. EH21 —2J 19
Ravensheugh Rd. EH21 —2J 19
Ravenswood Av. EH16 —3B 26
Redbraes Gro. EH7 —6C 8
Redbraes Pl. EH7 —6C 8
Redburn Rd. EH22 —3C 20
Redburn Rd. N. EH32
Redcroft St. EH22 —4G 27
Redford Av. EH13 —6K 23
Redford Bank. EH13 —6A 24
Redford Cres. EH13 —6A 24
Redford Dri. EH13 —6K 23
Redford Gdns. EH13 —6A 24
Redford Gro. EH13 —6B 24
Redford Loan. EH13 —6K 23
Redford Neuk. EH13 —6B 24
Redford Pl. EH13 —5B 24
Redford Rd. EH13 —5K 23
Redford Ter. EH13 —6A 24
Redford Wlk. EH13 —6A 24
Red Fox Cres. EH26 —2D 34
Redgauntlet Ter. EH16 —3C 26
Redhall Av. EH14 —2J 23
Redhall Bank Rd. EH14 —3K 23
Redhall Cres. EH14 —2J 23
Redhall Dri. EH14 —2J 23
Redhall Gdns. EH14 —2J 23
Redhall Gro. EH14 —2J 23
Redhall Ho. Dri. EH14 —3K 23
Redhall Pl. EH14 —2J 23
Redhall Rd. EH14 —2J 23
Redhall View. EH14 —3K 23
Redheugh Loan. EH23 —4H 35
Redheughs Av. EH12 —7C 12
Redheughs Muir. EH12 —7C 12
Redheughs Rigg. EH12 —6C 12
Redwood Gro. EH22 —7F 32
Redwood Wlk. EH22 —1F 35
Reed Dri. EH22 —7G 33
Reekies Ct. EH8 —4J 15 (6G 3)
Regent Pl. EH7 —2A 16
Regent Rd. EH1 & EH7 —2J 15 (2G 3)
Regent St. EH15 —3H 17
Regent St. La. EH15 —3H 17
Regent Ter. EH7 —2J 15 (2J 3)
Regent Ter. M. EH7 —2K 15 (1J 3)
Regis Ct. EH4 —6J 5
Register Pl. EH2 —2H 15 (2E 2)
Reid's Clo. EH8 —3K 15 (3J 3)
Reid's Ct. EH8 —3K 15 (3J 3)
Reid Ter. EH3 —1E 14
Relugas Gdns. EH9 —1J 25
Relugas Pl. EH9 —1J 25
Relugas Rd. EH9 —1J 25
Research Av. N. EH14 —3B 22
Research Av. One. EH14 —4B 22
Research Av. Two. EH14 —4B 22
Research Pk. Rd. EH14 —4B 22
Restalrig Av. EH7 —2C 16
Restalrig Cir. EH7 —7H 9
Restalrig Cres. EH7 —7H 9
Restalrig Dri. EH7 —7H 9
Restalrig Gdns. EH7 —1C 16
Restalrig Ho. Ct. EH7 —1C 16
Restalrig Pk. EH7 —7G 9
Restalrig Rd. EH6 & EH7 —6G 9
Restalrig Rd. S. EH7 —7H 9
Restalrig Ter. EH6 —6F 9
Riccarton Av. EH14 —7B 22
Riccarton Cres. EH14 —7C 22

Riccarton Dri. EH14 —7C 22
Riccarton Gro. EH14 —7C 22
Riccarton Mains Rd. EH14 —3B 22
Richmond La. EH8 —4J 15 (6G 3)
Richmond Pl. EH8 —4J 15 (5G 3)
Richmond Ter. EH11 —4E 14
Riddle's Ct. EH1 —4E 2
Riding Pk. EH4 —6J 5
Riego St. EH3 —4F 15 (6B 2)
Rigley Ter. EH32 —4C 20
Rillbank Cres. EH9 —6H 15
Rillbank Ter. EH9 —6H 15
Ringans Way. EH32 —3C 20 (off Inch View)
Ringwood Pl. EH16 —4B 26
Rintoul Pl. EH3 —1F 15
Riselaw Cres. EH10 —5E 24
Riselaw Pl. EH10 —4E 24
Riselaw Rd. EH10 —4E 24
Ritchie Pl. EH11 —6D 14
Riversdale Cres. EH12 —5A 14
Riversdale Gro. EH12 —4A 14
Riversdale Rd. EH12 —4A 14
Riverside. EH4 —4J 5
Riverside. EH28 —5A 10
Riverside Cotts. EH22 —5F 33
Riverside Gdns. EH21 —3D 18
Riverside Rd. EH30 —6F 5
Roanshead Rd. EH22 —5H 33
Robb's Loan. EH14 —7A 14
Robb's Loan Gro. EH14 —7A 14
Robert Burns Dri. EH16 —3A 26
Robert Burns M. EH22 —2J 33
Robert Smillie Av. EH22 —1K 35
Robertson Av. EH11 —6B 14
Robertson Av. EH32 —2E 20
Robertson Av. EH33 —6H 21
Robertson Bank. EH23
Robertson Dri. EH33 —5H 21
Robertson's Clo. EH1 —4J 15 (5G 3)
Robertson's Clo. EH22 —2F 33
Robertson's Ct. EH8 —3J 3
Rocheid Pk. EH4 —6J 7
Rocheid Path. EH3 —7A 8
Rochester Ter. EH10 —7E 14
Rockville Ter. EH19 —5A 32
Rodney St. EH7 —1G 15
Romero Pl. EH16 —6K 15
Ronaldson's Wharf. EH6 —5E 8
Rope Wlk. EH32 —3C 20
Rosabelle Rd. EH25 —1A 34
Rosebank Cotts. EH3 —4E 14
Rosebank Gdns. EH5 —5K 7
Rosebank Gro. EH5 —5K 7
Rosebank Rd. EH5 —5K 7
Rosebery Av. EH30 —6C 4
Rosebery Ct. EH30 —6C 4
Rosebery Cres. EH12 —4D 14
Rosebery Cres. EH23 —7H 35
Rosebery Cres. La. EH12 —4D 14
Roseburn Av. EH12 —4B 14
Roseburn Cliff. EH12 —4C 14
Roseburn Cres. EH12 —5B 14
Roseburn Dri. EH12 —4B 14
Roseburn Gdns. EH12 —4B 14
Roseburn Pl. EH12 —4B 14
Roseburn St. EH12 —5B 14
Roseburn Ter. EH12 —4B 14
Rose Ct. EH4 —6B 6
Rosefield Av. EH15 —3G 17
Rosefield Av. La. EH15 —3G 17
Rosefield Pl. EH15 —3G 17
Rosefield Pl. La. EH15 —3G 17

Rosefield St. EH15 —3G 17
Rose La. EH30 —5B 4
Rosemount Bldgs. EH3 —4E 14
Rosemount M. EH32 —2D 20
Roseneath Pl. EH9 —6H 15
Roseneath St. EH9 —6H 15
Roseneath Ter. EH9 —6H 15
Rose Pk. EH5 —5A 8
Rose St. EH2 —3F 15 (3B 2)
Rose St. N. La. EH2 (in six parts) —3F 15 (3B 2)
Rose St. S. La. EH2 (in four parts) —3F 15 (3B 2)
Rosevale Pl. EH6 —6G 9
Rosevale Ter. EH6 —6F 9
Roseville Gdns. EH5 —4B 8
Rosewell Rd. EH19 —7K 31
Ross Cres. EH33 —7H 21
Ross Gdns. EH9 —1J 25
Rossglen Ct. EH25 —1B 34
Rosshill Ter. EH30 —6D 4
Rossie Pl. EH7 —1K 15
Rosslyn Cres. EH6 —7D 8
Rosslyn Ter. EH6 —7D 8
Ross Pl. EH9 —1K 25
Ross Pl. EH22 —7G 33
Ross Rd. EH16 —2K 25
Rostbank St. EH5 —2H 7
Rothesay M. EH3 —3D 14
Rothesay Pl. EH3 —3E 14
Rothesay Pl. EH21 —3F 19
Rothesay Ter. EH3 —3E 14
Roull Gro. EH12 —6F 13
Roull Pl. EH12 —6G 13
Roull Rd. EH12 —6F 13
Rowallan Ct. EH12 —4C 12 (off Craigievar Wynd)
Rowan Gdns. EH19 —7A 32
Rowan Tree Av. EH14 —1G 29
Rowan Tree Gro. EH14 —2G 29
Rowantree Rd. FH22 —6K 33
Roxburgh Pl. EH8 —4J 15 (5G 3)
Roxburgh's Clo. EH1 —4E 2
Roxburgh St. EH8 —4J 15 (5G 3)
Royal Cir. EH3 —2F 15 (1B 2)
Royal Ct. EH26 —4A 34
Royal Cres. EH3 —1G 15
Royal Pk. Pl. EH8 —2B 16
Royal Pk. Ter. EH8 —2B 16
Royal Ter. EH7 —2J 15 (1G 3)
Royal Ter. M. EH7 —1J 3
Royston Mains Av. EH5 —4G 7
Royston Mains Clo. EH5 —4H 7
Royston Mains Cres. EH5 —4G 7
Royston Mains Gdns. EH5 —4H 7
Royston Mains Grn. EH5 —4H 7
Royston Mains Pl. EH5 —4G 7
Royston Mains Rd. EH5 —4H 7
Royston Mains St. EH5 —4G 7
Royston Ter. EH3 —6A 8
Rullion Grn. Av. EH26 —4A 34
Rullion Grn. Cres. EH26 —4A 34
Rullion Rd. EH26 —7A 34
Ruskin Pl. EH22 —1K 35
Russell Pl. EH5 —4A 8
Russell Rd. EH12 & EH11 —4C 14
Rustic Cotts. EH13 —6K 23
Rutherford Dri. EH16 —3B 26
Rutland Ct. EH3 —4F 15 (5A 2)
Rutland Ct. La. EH3 —4F 15 (5A 2)
Rutland Pl. EH2 —4A 2
Rutland Sq. EH1 —3F 15

Rutland Sq. EH2 —4A 2
Rutland St. EH1 —3F 15
Rutland St. EH2 —4A 2
Ryehill Av. EH6 —7G 9
Ryehill Gdns. EH6 —7G 9
Ryehill Gro. EH6 —7G 9
Ryehill Pl. EH6 —6G 9
Ryehill Ter. EH6 —6G 9

Saddletree Loan. EH16 —2C 26
St Albans Rd. EH9 —1H 25
St Andrew Pl. EH6 —6F 9
St Andrew Sq. EH2 —2H 15 (2E 2)
St Andrew St. EH22 —2F 33
St Anne's Ct. EH22 —1F 35
St Ann's Av. EH18 —7H 31
St Ann's Path. EH18 —7H 31
St Anthony La. EH6 —5E 8
St Anthony Pl. EH6 —5E 8
St Anthony St. EH6 —5E 8
St Bernard's Cres. EH4 —2E 14
St Bernard's Row. EH4 —1F 15
St Catherine's Gdns. EH12 —5J 13
St Catherine's Pl. EH9 —6J 15
St Clair Av. EH6 —7F 9
St Clair Cres. EH25 —1B 34
St Clair Pl. EH6 —7F 9
St Clair Rd. EH6 —7F 9
St Clair St. EH6 —7F 9
St Clair Ter. EH10 —2D 24
St Clement's Cres. EH21 —4K 19
St Clement's Gdns. N. EH21 —4K 19
St Clement's Gdns. S. EH21 —4K 19
St Clement's Ter. EH21 —4K 19
St Colme St. EH3 —2F 15 (2A 2)
St David's. EH22 —1F 35
St David's Pl. EH3 —4E 14
St David's Ter. EH3 —4E 14
St Fillans Ter. EH10 —2E 24
St Giles St. EH1 —3H 15 (4E 2)
St James Cen. EH1 —2H 15 (2F 3)
St James Pl. EH1 —2H 15 (1F 3)
St James's Gdns. EH26 —7B 34
St James's Sq. EH1 —2F 3
St James's View. EH26 —7B 34
St John's Av. EH12 —5G 13
St John's Cres. EH12 —5H 13
St John's Gdns. EH12 —5G 13
St John's Hill. EH8 —4J 15 (5H 3)
St John's Pl. EH12 —5E 12
St John's Ter. EH12 —5G 13
St John St. EH8 —3J 15 (4H 3)
St Katherine's Brae. EH16 —6A 26
St Katherine's Cres. EH16 —6A 26
St Katherine's Loan. EH16 —7B 26
St Kentigern Rd. EH26 —5A 34
St Kentigern Way. EH26 —6C 34
St Leonard's Bank. EH8 —5K 15 (7J 3)
St Leonard's Crag. EH8 —5K 15 (7J 3)
St Leonard's Hill. EH8 —4J 15 (6H 3)
St Leonard's La. EH8 —5J 15 (7H 3)

St Leonard's St. EH8
　—5J 15 (7H 3)
St Margaret's Rd. EH9 —7F 15
St Mark's La. EH15 —3H 17
St Mark's Pl. EH15 —3H 17
St Martin's La. EH33 —6H 21
St Mary's Pl. EH15 —4J 17
St Mary's Pl. La. EH15
　—3J 17
St Mary's St. EH1
　—3J 15 (4G 3)
St Michael's Av. EH21
　—3E 18
St Mungo's View. EH26
　—7C 34
St Ninian's Dri. EH12 —4F 13
St Ninian's Rd. EH12 —4F 13
St Ninian's Row. EH1 —2F 3
St Ninian's Ter. EH10 —2D 24
St Patrick Sq. EH8
　—5J 15 (7G 3)
St Patrick St. EH8
　—5J 15 (7G 3)
St Peter's Bldgs. EH3 —5E 14
St Peter's Pl. EH3 —5E 14
St Ringans Bldgs. EH32
　—2D 20
St Ronan's Ter. EH10 —2E 24
St Stephen Pl. EH3 —1F 15
St Stephen's Ct. EH11
　—3E 22
St Stephen St. EH3 —1F 15
St Teresa Pl. EH10 —7D 14
St Thomas Rd. EH9 —7H 15
St Vincent St. EH3 —1F 15
Salamanca Cres. EH26
　—3D 34
Salamander Pl. EH6 —5G 9
Salamander St. EH6 —5G 9
Salisbury Pl. EH9 —6J 15
Salisbury Rd. EH16 —6K 15
Salisbury View. EH22 —7J 33
Salmond Pl. EH7 —2A 16
Salters Gro. EH22 —1H 33
Salter's Rd. EH21 —6H 19
Salters Rd. EH22 —2H 33
　(in two parts)
Salters Ter. EH22 —2H 33
Saltire Ct. EH11 —5B 2
Salt Preston Pl. EH32 —2D 20
Salvesen Cres. EH4 —5D 6
Salvesen Gdns. EH4 —4E 6
Salvesen Gro. EH4 —3E 6
Salvesen Ter. EH4 —4E 6
Samoa Ter. EH26 —3D 34
Sanderson's Gro. EH33
　—5H 21
Sanderson's Wynd. EH33
　—5H 21
Sandford Gdns. EH15 —3G 17
Sand Port. EH6 —4F 9
Sandport Pl. EH6 —4E 8
Sandport St. EH6 —4E 8
Sandport Trading Est. EH6
　—4E 8
Sauchiebank. EH11 —5C 14
Saugh Cotts. EH22 —2F 35
Saughton Av. EH11 —7A 14
Saughton Cres. EH12 —5K 13
Saughton Gdns. EH12
　—5K 13
Saughton Gro. EH12 —5K 13
Saughtonhall Av. EH12
　—5K 13
Saughtonhall Av. W. EH12
　—5K 13
Saughtonhall Cir. EH12
　—5A 14
Saughtonhall Cres. EH12
　—5K 13
Saughtonhall Dri. EH12
　—5K 13
Saughtonhall Gdns. EH12
　—5A 14
Saughtonhall Gro. EH12
　—5A 14
Saughtonhall Pl. EH12
　—5K 13
Saughtonhall Ter. EH12
　—5A 14

Saughton Loan. EH12 —5K 13
Saughton Mains Av. EH11
　(in two parts)　　—7H 13
Saughton Mains Bank. EH11
　—7J 13
Saughton Mains Cotts. EH11
　—1H 23
(off Saughton Mains Gdns.)
Saughton Mains Dri. EH11
　—1H 23
Saughton Mains Gdns. EH11
　—1H 23
Saughton Mains Gro. EH11
　—1J 23
Saughton Mains Loan. EH11
　—1H 23
Saughton Mains Pk. EH11
　—7H 13
Saughton Mains Pl. EH11
　—1H 23
Saughton Mains St. EH11
　—7H 13
Saughton Mains Ter. EH11
　—7H 13
Saughton Pk. EH12 —5K 13
Saughton Rd. EH11 —7H 13
Saughton Rd. N. EH12
　—5G 13
Saunders Ct. EH12 —6E 12
Saunders St. EH3
　—2F 15 (1A 2)
Savile Pl. EH9 —1K 25
Savile Ter. EH9 —1K 25
Saxe Coburg Pl. EH3 —1F 15
Saxe Coburg St. EH3 —1F 15
Saxe Coburg Ter. EH3 —1F 15
(off Saxe Coburg St.)
Schaw Rd. EH32 —2F 21
School Brae. EH4 —4J 5
School Brae. EH18 —4K 31
School Grn. EH18 —4K 31
School La. EH32 —1A 20
School Wynd. EH28 —7B 10
Sciennes. EH9 —6J 15
Sciennes Gdns. EH9 —6J 15
Sciennes Hill Pl. EH9 —6J 15
Sciennes Ho. Pl. EH9 —6J 15
Sciennes Pl. EH9 —6J 15
Sciennes Rd. EH9 —6H 15
Scollon Av. EH19 —5B 32
Scone Gdns. EH8 —2C 16
Scotland St. EH3 —1G 15
Scotland St. La. E. EH3
　—1H 15
Scotland St. La. W. EH3
　—1G 15
Scotsman Bldgs. EH1 —3F 3
Scotstoun Av. EH30 —6C 4
Scotstoun Grn. EH30 —6C 4
Scotstoun Gro. EH30 —6C 4
Scotstoun Pk. EH30 —7C 4
Scott Rd. EH26 —4B 34
Scotway Cen., The. EH22
　—5K 27
Seacot. EH6 —6H 9
Seafield Av. EH6 —6H 9
Seafield Moor Rd. EH10 &
　EH25 —4A 30
Seafield Pl. EH6 —6H 9
Seafield Rd. EH6 —6H 9
Seafield Rd. EH25 —7A 30
Seafield Rd. E. EH15 —6K 9
Seafield St. EH6 —6J 9
Seafield Way. EH15 —7K 9
Seaforth Dri. EH4 —1A 14
Seaforth Ter. EH4 —1A 14
(off Queensferry Rd.)
Seaforth Ter. EH19 —7J 31
Sealcarr St. EH5 —3H 7
Seaport St. EH6 —5F 9
Seaview Cres. EH15 —4K 17
Seaview Ter. EH15 —4K 17
Second Gait. EH14 —4A 22
Second St. EH22 —2G 35
Semple St. EH3
　—4F 15 (6A 2)
Seton Ct. EH32 —1C 20
Seton Ct. EH33 —7G 21
Seton Pl. EH9 —6J 15
Seton St. EH32 —1B 20

Seton Sands Residential
　Caravan Site. EH32 —1K 21
Seton View. EH32 —1C 20
Seton Wynd. EH32 —1C 20
Seventh St. EH22 —1G 35
Shadepark Cres. EH22
　—1G 33
Shadepark Dri. EH22 —1G 33
Shadopark Gdns. EH22
　—1G 33
Shaftesbury Pk. EH11
　—7C 14
Shandon Cres. EH11 —7C 14
Shandon Pl. EH11 —7C 14
Shandon Rd. EH11 —7C 14
Shandon St. EH11 —7C 14
Shandon Ter. EH11 —7C 14
Shandwick Pl. EH2 —4E 14
Shanter Way. EH16 —3A 26
Sharpdale Loan. EH16
　—2B 26
Shaw Pl. EH22 —5J 33
Shaws Ct. EH26 —2D 34
Shaw's Pl. EH7 —7D 8
Shaw Sq. EH1 —1H 15
Shaw's St. EH7 —7D 8
Shaw's Ter. EH7 —7D 8
Sheriff Bank. EH6 —5E 8
Sheriff Brae. EH6 —5E 8
Sheriffhall Mains Cotts. EH22
　—6K 27
Sheriff Pk. EH6 —5E 8
Sherwood Av. EH19 —7B 32
Sherwood Cotts. EH19
　—7C 32
Sherwood Ct. EH19 —7B 32
Sherwood Cres. EH19
　—7B 32
Sherwood Dri. EH19 —7B 32
Sherwood Gro. EH19 —7C 32
Sherwood Ind. Est. EH19
　—6B 32
Sherwood Loan. EH19
　—7B 32
Sherwood Pk. EH19 —7B 32
Sherwood Pl. EH19 —7B 32
Sherwood Ter. EH19 —7B 32
Sherwood View. EH19 —7B 32
Sherwood Wlk. EH19 —7C 32
Sherwood Way. EH19 —7B 32
Shore. EH6 —5F 9
Shore Pl. EH6 —5F 9
Shore Rd. EH30 —5B 4
Shorthope St. EH21 —2E 18
Shrub Mt. EH15 —2G 17
Shrub Pl. EH7 —7D 8
Shrub Pl. La. EH7 —7D 8
Sienna Gdns. EH9 —6J 15
Sighthill Av. EH11 —2G 23
Sighthill Bank. EH11 —2F 23
Sighthill Ct. EH11 —2F 23
Sighthill Cres. EH11 —3F 23
Sighthill Dri. EH11 —3F 23
Sighthill Gdns. EH11 —2F 23
Sighthill Grn. EH11 —2F 23
Sighthill Gro. EH11 —2G 23
Sighthill Ind. Est. EH11
　—1D 22
Sighthill Loan. EH11 —2F 23
Sighthill Neuk. EH11 —2F 23
Sighthill Pk. EH11 —2F 23
Sighthill Pl. EH11 —2F 23
Sighthill Rise. EH11 —3F 23
Sighthill Rd. EH11 —3F 23
Sighthill Shopping Cen. EH11
　—2F 23
Sighthill St. EH11 —3F 23
Sighthill Ter. EH11 —2F 23
Sighthill View. EH11 —2F 23
Sighthill Wynd. EH11 —2F 23
Silverburn Dri. EH26 —5A 34
Silverknowes Av. EH4 —6B 6
Silverknowes Bank. EH4
　—6C 6
Silverknowes Brae. EH4
　—6C 6
Silverknowes Ct. EH4 —6C 6
Silverknowes Cres. EH4
　—6C 6
Silverknowes Dell. EH4 —6C 6

Silverknowes Dri. EH4 —6C 6
Silverknowes Eastway. EH4
　—6C 6
Silverknowes Gdns. EH4
　—5C 6
Silverknowes Grn. EH4 —6D 6
Silverknowes Gro. EH4 —5C 6
Silverknowes Hill. EH4 —6C 6
Silverknowes Loan. EH4
　—6C 6
Silverknowes Midway. EH4
　—6D 6
Silverknowes Neuk. EH4
　—7D 6
Silverknowes Parkway. EH4
　—5C 6
Silverknowes Pl. EH4 —5C 6
Silverknowes Rd. EH4 —4B 6
Silverknowes Rd. E. EH4
　—6C 6
Silverknowes Rd. S. EH4
　—7C 6
Silverknowes Southway. EH4
　—6D 6
Silverknowes Ter. EH4 —6B 6
Silverknowes View. EH4
　—6D 6
Simon Sq. EH8
　—4J 15 (6G 3)
Simpson's Bldgs. EH4 —5C 6
Sir Harry Lauder Rd. EH15
　—2F 17
Sir Walter Scott Pend. EH32
　—2D 20
Sir William Fraser Homes.
　EH13 —5J 23
Sixth St. EH22 —1F 35
Skeltie Muir Av. EH19
　—7K 31
Skeltie Muir Ct. EH19 —7K 31
Skeltie Muir Gro. EH19
　—7A 32
Slaeside. EH14 —4E 28
Slateford Rd. EH14 & EH11
　—2A 24
Sleigh Dri. EH7 —1B 16
Sleigh Gdns. EH7 —1C 16
Sloan St. EH6 —7E 8
Smeaton Gro. EH21 —5F 19
Smithfield St. EH11 —6B 14
Smith's Pl. EH6 —6E 8
Smithy Grn. Av. EH22
　—5H 27
Society Rd. EH30 —4A 4
Solicitors Bldgs. EH1 —5F 3
Somerset Pl. EH6 —6F 9
Somerville Gdns. EH30 —7D 4
Sour Howe. EH10 —7D 24
Southbank. EH4 —6B 6
Southbank Ct. EH4 —6B 6
S. Barnton Av. EH4 —7B 6
S. Beechwood. EH12 —5J 13
South Bri. EH1 —3H 15 (4F 3)
S. Charlotte St. EH2
　—3F 15 (3B 2)
S. Clerk St. EH8 —5J 15
S. College St. EH8
　—4H 15 (5F 3)
South Cres. EH32 —3E 20
S. Doors. EH32 —1A 20
S. E. Circus Pl. EH3
　—2F 15 (1B 2)
S. E. Thistle St. La. EH2
　—2D 2
S. Ettrick Rd. EH10 —7D 14
Southfield Bank. EH15
　—5F 17
Southfield Farm Gro. EH15
　—4E 16
Southfield Gdns. E. EH15
　—4F 17
Southfield Gdns. W. EH15
　—4F 17
Southfield Loan. EH15
　—5F 17
Southfield Pl. EH15 —3G 17
Southfield Rd. E. EH15
　—5F 17
Southfield Rd. W. EH15
　—5E 16

Southfield Sq. EH15 —5F 17
Southfield Ter. EH15 —5F 17
Southfield Vs. EH15 —4G 17
S. Fort St. EH6 —5D 8
S. Gayfield La. EH1 —1J 15
S. Gillsland Rd. EH10
　—1D 24
S. Grange Av. EH32 —4C 20
S. Gray's Clo. EH1
　—3J 15 (4G 3)
S. Gray St. EH9 7K 15
S. Groathill Av. EH4 —1A 14
S. Gyle Access. EH12 —7E 12
S. Gyle B'way. EH12 —6B 12
S. Gyle Cres. EH12 —7C 12
S. Gyle Cres. La. EH12
　—7D 12
S. Gyle Gdns. EH12 —6D 12
S. Gyle Ind. Est. EH12
　—7D 12
S. Gyle Loan. EH12 —6D 12
S. Gyle Mains. EH12 —6D 12
S. Gyle Pk. EH12 —6D 12
S. Gyle Rd. EH12 —6D 12
S. Gyle Wynd. EH12 —6E 12
Southhouse Av. EH17
　—7B 26
Southhouse B'way. EH17
　—1E 30
Southhouse Cres. EH17
　—1E 30
Southhouse Gdns. EH17
　—1E 30
Southhouse Gro. EH17
　—1E 30
Southhouse Loan. EH17
　—7B 26
Southhouse Medway. EH17
　—7B 26
Southhouse Path. EH17
　—7B 26
Southhouse Rd. EH17
　—7B 26
Southhouse Sq. EH17
　—1E 30
Southhouse Ter. EH17
　—7C 26
S. Lauder Rd. EH9 —7J 15
S. Laverockbank Av. EH5
　—4B 8
Southlawn Ct. EH4 —6B 6
S. Learmonth Av. EH4
　—2D 14
S. Learmonth Gdns. EH4
　—2D 14
S. Lorimer Pl. EH32 —1G 21
S. Lorne Pl. EH6 —7E 8
S. Maybury. EH12 —5C 12
S. Meadow Wlk. EH9 —5G 15
S. Mellis Pk. EH8 —3K 16
S. Oswald Rd. EH9 —1G 25
S. Oxford St. EH8 —6K 15
Southpark. EH6 —6C 8
　(Bonnington)
South Pk. EH6 —4C 8
　(Newhaven)
S. St Andrew St. EH2
　—2H 15 (2E 2)
S. St David St. EH2
　—3H 15 (2E 2)
S. Scotstoun. EH30 —7C 4
S. Seton Pk. EH32 —1G 21
S. Sloan St. EH6 —7E 8
South St. EH21 —2D 18
South St. EH22 —2F 33
S. Trinity Rd. EH5 —5A 8
S. View. EH32 —3E 20
S. W. Thistle St. La. EH2
　—2C 2
Soutra Ct. EH16 —6B 26
Spalding Cres. EH22 —2G 33
Spa Pl. EH15 —2G 17
Speedwell Av. EH22 —4G 27
Spencer Pl. EH5 —4A 8
Spence St. EH16 —6K 15
Spey St. EH7 —7D 8
Spey St. La. EH7 —7D 8
(off Spey St. M.)
Spey St. M. EH7 —7D 8
Spey Ter. EH7 —7D 8

Spier's Pl. EH6 —5E **8**
Spinney, The. EH17 —6D **26**
Spittalfield Cres. EH8 —5J **15**
Spittal St. EH3
—4G **15** (6B **2**)
Spittal St. La. EH3
—4G **15** (5C **2**)
Spottiswoode Rd. EH9
—6G **15**
Spottiswoode St. EH9
—6G **15**
Springfield EH6 —6E **8**
Springfield Bldgs. EH6 —6E **8**
Springfield Cres. EH30 —5A **4**
Springfield La. EH6 —6E **8**
Springfield Pl. EH23 —7J **35**
Springfield Pl. EH25 —1B **34**
Springfield Rd. EH30 —5A **4**
Springfield St. EH6 —6E **8**
Springfield View. EH30 —5A **4**
Spring Gdns. EH8 —2A **16**
Springvalley Gdns. EH10
—1E **24**
Springvalley Ter. EH10
—1E **24**
Springwell Pl. EH11 —5D **14**
Springwell Ter. EH30 —5B 4
(off Hopetoun Rd.)
Springwood Pk. EH16 —4B **26**
Spruce Wlk. EH20 —6B **30**
Spylaw Av. EH13 —5H **23**
Spylaw Bank Rd. EH13
—5H **23**
Spylaw Ho. EH13 —6J **23**
Spylaw Rd. EH13 —5H **23**
Spylaw Rd. EH10 —7D **14**
Spylaw St. EH13 —6J **23**
Square, The. EH22 —4H **27**
(Danderhall)
Square, The. EH22 —1G **35**
(Newtongrange)
Square, The. EH26 —7C **34**
Square, The. EH29 —2B **10**
Stable La. EH10 —7E **14**
Stafford St. EH3 —3E **14**
Stair Pk. EH12 —4A **14**
Stair Pk. EH33 —5F **21**
Standingstane Rd. EH30
—7E **4**
Stanedykehead. EH16 —6K **25**
Stanhope Pl. EH12 —4C **14**
Stanhope St. EH12 —4C **14**
Stanley Av. EH25 —7B **30**
Stanley Pl. EH7 —2A **16**
Stanley Rd. EH6 —4B **8**
Stanley St. EH15 —4G **17**
Stanwell St. EH6 —6E **8**
Stapeley Av. EH7 —1E **16**
Starbank Rd. EH5 —4B **8**
Stark's Cotts. EH13 —5C **24**
Station Brae. EH15 —3G **17**
Station Loan. EH14 —2E **28**
Station Rd. EH12 —5G **13**
Station Rd. EH20 —5F **31**
Station Rd. EH21 —3E **18**
Station Rd. EH22 —3D **32**
(Dalkeith)
Station Rd. EH22 —1F **35**
(Newtongrange)
Station Rd. EH23 —7H **35**
Station Rd. EH25 —1B **34**
Station Rd. EH28 —5C **10**
Station Rd. EH29 —1B **10**
Station Rd. EH30 —5C **4**
Station Rd. EH32 —4E **20**
Station Ter. EH29 —2B **10**
Stead's Pl. EH6 —6E **8**
Steele Av. EH22 —7K **33**
Steel's Pl. EH10 —1F **25**
Steil Gro. EH33 —7H **21**
Steils, The. EH10 —3C **24**
Stenhouse Av. EH11 —6J **13**
Stenhouse Av. W. EH11
—7J **13**
Stenhouse Cotts. EH11
—7J **13**
Stenhouse Cres. EH11
—7J **13**
Stenhouse Cross. EH11
(off Stenhouse Dri.) —7J 13
Stenhouse Dri. EH11 —7H **13**

Stenhouse Gdns. EH11
—7J **13**
Stenhouse Gdns. N. EH11
—7J **13**
Stenhouse Gro. EH11 —7J **13**
Stenhouse Mill Cres. EH11
—1K **23**
Stenhouse Mill La. EH11
—1K **23**
Stenhouse Mill Wynd. EH11
—1K **23**
Stenhouse Pl. E. EH11 —7J **13**
Stenhouse Pl. W. EH11
—7J **13**
Stenhouse Rd. EH11 —1J **23**
Stenhouse St. E. EH11
—7J **13**
Stenhouse St. W. EH11
—7H **13**
Stenhouse Ter. EH11 —7H **13**
Stennis Gdns. EH17 —5C **26**
Stevenlaw's Clo. EH1
(in two parts) —3H **15** (4F **3**)
Stevenson Av. EH11 —6A **14**
Stevenson Dri. EH11 —7J **13**
Stevenson Gro. EH11 —6A **14**
Stevenson La. EH22 —2G **35**
Stevenson Pl. EH18 —7G **31**
Stevenson Rd. EH11 —6A **14**
Stevenson Rd. EH26 —3D **34**
Stevenson Ter. EH11 —6A **14**
Stewart Av. EH14 —2G **29**
Stewart Clark Av. EH30 —6C **4**
Stewart Cres. EH14 —1G **29**
Stewartfield. EH6 —6C **8**
Stewart Gdns. EH14 —1G **29**
Stewart Pl. EH14 —2G **29**
Stewart Pl. EH29 —1B **10**
Stewart Ter. EH14 —2G **29**
Stewart Ter. EH11 —6B **14**
Stewart Ter. EH30 —5A **4**
(in two parts)
Stirling Rd. EH3 —4A **8**
Stobhill Ct. EH22 & EH23
—2G **35**
Stockbridge Ho. EH4 —1E 14
(off Cheyne St.)
Stone Av. EH22 —7J **33**
Stone Pl. EH22 —1J **35**
Stoneybank Av. EH21 —4C **18**
Stoneybank Ct. EH21 —3C **18**
Stoneybank Cres. EH21
—4D **18**
Stoneybank Dri. EH21 —4D **18**
Stoneybank Gdns. EH21
—3C **18**
Stoneybank Gdns. N. EH21
—3D **18**
Stoneybank Gdns. S. EH21
—4D **18**
Stoneybank Gro. EH21
—4D **18**
Stoneybank Pl. EH21 —4D **18**
Stoneybank Rd. EH21 —4D **18**
Stoneybank Ter. EH21
—4D **18**
Stoney Croft Rd. EH30 —5B **4**
Stoneyflatts. EH30 —6A **4**
Stoneyflatts Cres. EH30 —5A **4**
Stoneyflatts Pk. EH30 —6A **4**
Stoneyhill Av. EH21 —3C **18**
Stoneyhill Ct. EH21 —3C **18**
Stoneyhill Cres. EH21 —3C **18**
Stoneyhill Dri. EH21 —3C **18**
Stoneyhill Farm Rd. EH21
(in two parts) —3D **18**
Stoneyhill Gro. EH21 —3C **18**
Stoneyhill Pl. EH21 —3C **18**
Stoneyhill Rise. EH21 —3C **18**
Stoneyhill Rd. EH21 —3C **18**
Stoneyhill Ter. EH21 —3C **18**
Stoneyhill Wynd. EH21
—3C **18**
Stoneypath. EH14 —3K **23**
Strachan Gdns. EH4 —1J **13**
Strachan Rd. EH4 —1J **13**
Straiton Junction. EH17
—2E **30**
Straiton La. EH15 —3H **17**
Straiton Mains. EH20 —4D **30**

Straiton Pk. Caravan Pk. EH20
—4C **30**
Straiton Pl. EH15 —2H **17**
Straiton Pl. Loan. EH15
—3H **17**
Straiton Retail Pk. EH20
—4D **30**
Straiton Rd. EH17 & EH20
—1D **30**
Strathalmond Ct. EH4 —7G **5**
Strathalmond Grn. EH4
—7G **5**
Strathalmond Pk. EH4
—1B **12**
Strathalmond Rd. EH4
—1B **12**
Strathearn Pl. EH9 —7F **15**
Strathearn Rd. EH9 —7G **15**
Strathesk Gro. EH26 —5D **34**
Strathesk Pl. EH26 —5D **34**
Strathesk Rd. EH26 —5D **34**
Strathfillan Rd. EH9 —7G **15**
Strawberry Bank. EH22
—4D **32**
Stuart Ct. EH12 —3D **12**
Stuart Cres. EH12 —3D **12**
Stuart Grn. EH12 —3D **12**
Stuart Pk. EH12 —3D **12**
Stuart Sq. EH12 —3D **12**
Stuart Wynd. EH12 —3D **12**
Succoth Av. EH12 —3B **14**
Succoth Ct. EH12 —3B **14**
Succoth Gdns. EH12 —3B **14**
Succoth Pk. EH12 —3A **14**
Succoth Pl. EH12 —3B **14**
Suffolk Rd. EH16 —1K **25**
Sugarhouse Clo. EH8 —4H **3**
Summer Bank. EH3 —1G **15**
Summerfield Gdns. EH6
—6G **9**
Summerfield Pl. EH6 —6G **9**
Summerhall. EH9 —5J **15**
Summerhall Pl. EH10 —6J **15**
(off Summerhall)
Summerhall Sq. EH9 —6J **15**
Summerlee. EH32 —3G **20**
Summer Pl. EH3 —7A **8**
Summerside Pl. EH6 —5C **8**
Summerside St. EH6 —5C **8**
Summertrees Ct. EH16
—3B **26**
Sunbury M. EH4 —3D **14**
Sunbury Pl. EH4 —3D **14**
Sunbury St. EH4 —3D **14**
Sunnybank. EH7 —2B **16**
Sunnybank Pl. EH7 —2B **16**
Sunnybank Ter. EH7 —2A 16
(off Lwr. London Rd.)
Sunnyside. EH7 —1A **16**
Surgeon's Hall. EH8 —5G **3**
Surrey Pl. EH12 —4C **14**
Sutherland St. EH12 —4C **14**
Suttieslea Cres. EH22 —7H **33**
Suttieslea Dri. EH22 —7H **33**
Suttieslea Pl. EH22 —7H **33**
Suttieslea Rd. EH22 —7H **33**
Suttieslea Wlk. EH22 —7H **33**
Swan Cres. EH23 —5H **35**
Swanfield. EH6 —5E **8**
Swan Rd. EH33 —7G **21**
Swan Spring Av. EH10
—5D **24**
Swanston Av. EH10 —7E **24**
Swanston Cres. EH10 —7E **24**
Swanston Dri. EH10 —7F **25**
Swanston Gdns. EH10 —7E **24**
Swanston Grn. EH10 —7E **24**
Swanston Gro. EH10 —7F **25**
Swanston Loan. EH10 —7E **24**
Swanston Muir. EH10 —7C **24**
Swanston Pk. EH10 —7E **24**
Swanston Pl. EH10 —7E **24**
Swanston Rd. EH10 —7D **24**
Swanston Row. EH10 —7E **24**
Swanston Ter. EH10 —7F **25**
Swanston View. EH10 —7E **24**
Swanston Way. EH10 —7E **24**
Sycamore Ct. EH12 —5F **13**
Sycamore Gdns. EH12
—5G **13**

Sycamore Path. EH20 —6B 30
(off Nivensknowe
Caravan Pk.)
Sycamore Rd. EH22 —7K **33**
Sycamore Ter. EH12 —5G **13**
Sydney Pk. EH7 —1E **16**
Sydney Pl. EH7 —1E **16**
Sydney Ter. EH7 —1E **16**
Sylvan Pl. EH9 —6H **15**
Tait Dri. EH26 —6C **34**
Tait St. EH22 —2F **33**
Talisman Pl. EH16 —3B **26**
Tanfield. EH3 —7B **8**
Tantallon Pl. EH9 —6H **15**
Tarvit St. EH3 —5F **15** (7B **2**)
Taylor Gdns. EH6 —5E **8**
Taylor Pl. EH7 —2A 16
(off Lwr. London Rd.)
Taylor Pl. EH22 —3H **33**
Tay St. EH11 —6D **14**
Telfer Subway. EH11 —5D **14**
Telferton. EH7 —2F **17**
Telford Cotts. EH26 —7C **34**
Telford Dri. EH4 —7G **7**
Telford Gdns. EH4 —7G **7**
Telford Pl. EH4 —7G **7**
Telford Rd. EH4 —1K **13**
Templeland Gro. EH12
—4F **13**
Templeland Rd. EH12 —4E **12**
Temple Pk. Cres. EH11
—6D **14**
Tennant St. EH6 —6F **8**
Tenth St. EH22 —7G **33**
Terregles. EH26 —5A **34**
Teviotdale Pl. EH3 —7A **8**
Teviot Gro. EH26 —4C **34**
Teviot Pl. EH8 —4H **15** (6E **2**)
Third Gait. EH14 —4A **22**
Third St. EH22 —1G **35**
Thirlestane La. EH9 —7G **15**
Thirlestane Rd. EH9 —6G **15**
Thistle Ct. EH2 —2D **2**
Thistle Pl. EH11 —6E **14**
Thistle St. EH2 —2G **15** (2C **2**)
Thistle St. N. E. La. EH2
—2G **15**
Thistle St. N. W. La. EH2
—2G **15**
Thistle St. S. E. La. EH2
—2G **15**
Thistle St. S. W. La. EH2
—2G **15**
Thomas Fraser Ct. EH6 —4E 8
(off Admiralty St.)
Thomson Cres. EH14 —7D **22**
Thomson Cres. EH32 —1A **20**
Thomson Dri. EH14 —7D **22**
Thomson Rd. EH14 —7D **22**
Thomson's Ct. EH1 —5D **2**
Thomson's Ct. EH8 —3K **3**
Thorburn Gro. EH13 —6A **24**
Thorburn Rd. EH13 —6K **23**
Thornburn Ter. EH26 —7B **34**
Thornhall Cotts. EH22 —1G **33**
Thorntree Cres. EH32 —3F **21**
Thorntree Side. EH6 —7H **9**
Thorntree St. EH6 —6F **9**
Thornville Ter. EH6 —7F **9**
Thornybank. EH22 —1H **33**
Thornybank Ind. Est. EH22
—1J **33**
Thornybauk. EH3 —5F **15**
(in two parts)
Threipmuir Av. EH14 —5E **28**
Threipmuir Gdns. EH14
—5E **28**
Threipmuir Pl. EH14 —5E **28**
Timber Bush. EH6 —4F **9**
Timmins Ct. EH28 —7B **10**
Tinto Pl. EH6 —6D **8**
Tipperlin Rd. EH10 —7E **14**
Toddshill Rd. EH29 —2A **10**
Tolbooth Wynd. EH6 —5E **8**
Torduff Rd. EH13 —7H **23**

Torphichen Pl. EH3 —4E **14**
Torphichen Pl. La. EH3
(off Torphichen Pl.) —4E **14**
Torphichen St. EH3 —4E **14**
Torphin Rd. EH13 —7G **23**
Torrance Pk. EH4 —2E **12**
Torsonce Rd. EH22 —3E **32**
Toward Ct. EH12 —4C 12
(off Craigievar Wynd)
Tower Pl. EH6 —4F **9**
Tower St. EH6 —4F **9**
Tower St. La. EH6 —4F **9**
Trafalgar La. EH6 —5D **8**
Trafalgar St. EH6 —5D **8**
Tranent By-Pass. EH33
—6D **20**
Traprain Ter. EH20 —6F **31**
Traquair Pk. E. EH12 —5H **13**
Traquair Pk. W. EH12
—5G **13**
Trelawney Ter. EH26 —3D **34**
Trench Knowe. EH10 —7E **24**
Tressilian Gdns. EH16
—3B **26**
Trinity Ct. EH5 —5A **8**
Trinity Cres. EH5 —3A **8**
Trinity Gro. EH5 —4A **8**
Trinity Mains. EH5 —5A **8**
Trinity Pk. Ho. EH5 —5A **8**
Trinity Rd. EH5 —4A **8**
Tron Sq. EH1 —4G **3**
Trunk's Clo. EH1 —4G **3**
Tryst Pk. EH10 —7D **24**
Tunnel, The. EH14 —3J **23**
Turner Av. EH14 —2D **28**
Turner Pk. EH14 —2E **28**
Turnhouse Farm Rd. EH12
—2J **11**
Turnhouse Rd. EH12 —2H **11**
Turret Gdns. EH32 —4D **20**
Tweedale Ct. EH1 —4G **3**
Tweedsmuir Ho. EH16
—1G **27**
Tyler's Acre Av. EH12
—6G **13**
Tyler's Acre Gdns. EH12
—6G **13**
Tyler's Acre Rd. EH12
—6G **13**
Tynecastle La. EH11 —6C **14**
Tynecastle Ter. EH11 —6C **14**
Ulster Cres. EH8 —3C **16**
Ulster Dri. EH8 —3D **16**
Ulster Gdns. EH8 —4D **16**
Ulster Gro. EH8 —4D **16**
Ulster Ter. EH8 —4D **16**
Union Pk. EH19 —6A **32**
Union Pl. EH1 —1G **3**
Union St. EH1 —1H **15**
Up. Bow. EH1 —3H **15** (4E **2**)
Up. Broomieknowe. EH18
—6K **31**
Up. Coltbridge Ter. EH12
—3C **14**
Up. Craigour. EH17 —3D **26**
Up. Craigour Way. EH17
—3D **26**
Up. Cramond Ct. EH4 —6J **5**
Up. Damside. EH4 —3D **14**
Up. Dean Ter. EH4 —2E **14**
Up. Gilmore Pl. EH3 —5F **15**
Up. Gilmore Ter. EH3 —5F **15**
Up. Gray St. EH9 —6J **15**
Up. Greenside La. EH1
—2J **15** (1G **3**)
Up. Grove Pl. EH3 —5E **14**

Valleyfield Rd. EH26 —7C **34**
Valleyfield St. EH3 —5F **15**
Valleyfield View. EH26
—7C **34**
Vanburgh Pl. EH6 —6F **9**
Vandeleur Av. EH7 —1E **16**
Vandeleur Gro. EH7 —2F **17**
Vandeleur Pl. EH7 —1E **16**
Veitch's Sq. EH4 —1F **15**
Vennel. EH1 —4G **15** (5D **2**)

Vennel. EH14 —2J **23**
(off Longstone Rd.)
Vennel, The. EH30 —5C **4**
Ventnor Pl. EH9 —7A **16**
Ventnor Ter. EH9 —7K **15**
Vexhim Pk. EH15 —6H **17**
Victoria Gdns. EH22 —7E **32**
Victoria Rd. EH22 —7E **32**
Victoria St. EH1
　　　　—4H **15** (5E **2**)
Victoria St. EH23 —5G **35**
Victoria St. EH24 —7F **35**
Victoria Ter. EH1 —5D **2**
Victoria Ter. EH21 —2G **19**
Victor Pk. Ter. EH12 —4F **13**
Viewbank Av. EH19 —5B **32**
Viewbank Cres. EH19 —5B **32**
Viewbank Dri. EH19 —5B **32**
Viewbank Rd. EH19 —5A **32**
Viewbank View. EH19 —5B **32**
Viewcraig Gdns. EH8
　　　　—3J **15** (4H **3**)
Viewcraig St. EH8
　　　　—4J **15** (4H **3**)
Viewfield. EH19 —5C **32**
Viewfield Rd. EH14 —5G **23**
Viewforth. EH11 & EH10
　　　　—5E **14**
Viewforth. EH32 —1B **20**
Viewforth Gdns. EH10 —6F **15**
Viewforth Gdns. EH33
　　　　—6G **21**
Viewforth Pl. EH30 —6B **4**
Viewforth Rd. EH30 —5B **4**
Viewforth Sq. EH10 —6E **14**
Viewforth Ter. EH10 —6E **14**
Viewforth Ter. EH33 —6G **21**
Viewpark Gdns. EH19 —5A **32**
Villa Rd. EH30 —5B **4**
Violet Ter. EH11 —6C **14**
Vivian Ter. EH4 —7C **6**
Vogrie Cres. S. EH23 —6J **35**
Vogrie Pl. EH23 —6J **35**
Vogrie Rd. EH23 —7J **35**
Vorlich Cres. EH26 —4D **34**

Waddell Pl. EH6 —6E **8**
Wadingburn La. EH18
　　　　—4J **31**
Wadingburn Rd. EH18
　　　　—5H **31**
Wakefield Av. EH7 —1F **17**
Walker Cres. EH22 —4C **32**
Walker Dri. EH30 —5A **4**
Walker Pl. EH18 —7H **31**
Walkers Ct. EH14 —3G **23**
Walkers Rigg. EH14 —3G **23**
Walker St. EH3 —3E **14**
Walkers Wynd. EH14 —3G **23**
Walker Ter. EH11 —4E **14**
Wallace Cres. EH25 —1B **34**
Wallace Pl. EH33 —5G **21**
Wallyford Ind. Est. EH21
　　　　—4K **19**
Walter Scott Av. EH16 —3B **26**
(in two parts)
Warden's Clo. EH1 —5E **2**
Wardie Av. EH5 —5K **7**
Wardieburn Dri. EH5 —4J **7**
Wardieburn Pl. E. EH5 —4J **7**
Wardieburn Pl. N. EH5 —4J **7**
Wardieburn Pl. S. EH5 —4J **7**
Wardieburn Pl. W. EH5 —4H **7**
Wardieburn St. E. EH5 —4J **7**
Wardieburn St. W. EH5
　　　　—4H **7**
Wardieburn Ter. EH5 —4J **7**
Wardie Cres. EH5 —4K **7**
Wardie Dell. EH5 —4K **7**
Wardie Field. EH5 —4J **7**
Wardie Gro. EH5 —4J **7**
Wardie Ho. La. EH5 —4K **7**
Wardie Pk. EH5 —5K **7**
Wardie Rd. EH5 —5K **7**
Wardie Sq. EH5 —4K **7**
Wardie Steps. EH5 —4K **7**
Wardlaw Pl. EH11 —6C **14**
Wardlaw St. EH11 —6C **14**

Wardlaw Ter. EH11 —6C **14**
Wardrop's Ct. EH1 —4E **2**
Warrender Pk. Cres. EH9
　　　　—6F **15**
Warrender Pk. Rd. EH9
　　　　—6G **15**
Warrender Pk. Ter. EH9
　　　　—6G **15**
Warriston Av. EH3 —6B **8**
Warriston Cres. EH3 —7B **8**
Warriston Dri. EH3 —6A **8**
Warriston Gdns. EH3 —6A **8**
Warriston Gro. EH3 —6A **8**
Warriston Pl. EH3 —7B **8**
(off Inverleith Row.)
Warriston Rd. EH3 & EH7
　　　　—7B **8**
Warriston's Clo. EH1 —4E **2**
Warriston Ter. EH3 —6A **8**
Washington La. EH11 —5D **14**
Washington St. EH11 —5D **14**
Waterloo Pl. EH1
　　　　—2H **15** (2F **3**)
Waterloo Rd. EH13 —7H **21**
Water of Leith Walkway. EH4
(off Malta Ter.) —1F **15**
Water's Clo. EH6 —5F **9**
Water St. EH6 —5F **9**
Watertoun Rd. EH9 —1J **25**
Watson Cres. EH11 —6D **14**
Watson's Bldgs. EH4 —7C **6**
Watson St. EH26 —6C **34**
Watt Gro. EH22 —1K **35**
Watt Pk. EH22 —2G **35**
Watt's Clo. EH21 —2D **18**
Wauchope Av. EH16 —7E **16**
Wauchope Cres. EH16
　　　　—7E **16**
Wauchope Ho. EH16 —1F **27**
Wauchope Pl. EH16 —7E **16**
(in two parts)
Wauchope Rd. EH16 —7F **17**
Wauchope Sq. EH16 —7F **17**
Wauchope Ter. EH16 —7E **16**
Waugh Path. EH19 —5C **32**
Waulkmill Dri. EH26 —7C **34**
Waulkmill Loan. EH14
　　　　—2G **29**
Waulkmill Rd. EH26 —6C **34**
Waulkmill View. EH26 —7C **34**
Waverley Bri. EH1
　　　　—3H **15** (3E **2**)
Waverley Ct. EH19 —6B **32**
Waverley Cres. EH19 —6B **32**
Waverley Dri. EH19 —6B **32**
Waverley Mkt. EH2
　　　　—3H **15** (3E **2**)
Waverley Pk. EH8 —2A **16**
Waverley Pk. EH19 —6B **32**
Waverley Pk. EH22 —7J **33**
Waverley Pk. Ter. EH8
　　　　—2A **16**
Waverley Pl. EH7 —2A **16**
Waverley Rd. EH19 —6B **32**
Waverley Rd. EH22 —3E **32**
Waverley Steps. EH2 —3F **3**
Waverley St. EH22 —1J **35**
Waverley Ter. EH19 —6B **32**
Waverley Ter. EH22 —7J **33**
Weavers Knowe Cres. EH14
　　　　—7B **22**
Webster's Land. EH1 —5C **2**
Wedderburn Ter. EH21
　　　　—4F **19**
Wee Brae. EH18 —4K **31**
Weir Ct. EH11 —2F **23**
(off Sighthill Bank)
Weir Cres. EH22 —1J **35**
Well Ct. EH4 —3E **14**
Wellflats Rd. EH29 —2B **10**
Wellington Cotts. EH22
　　　　—7B **18**
Wellington Pl. EH6 —6F **9**
Wellington St. EH7 —1K **15**
Well Wynd. EH21 —6H **21**
Wemyss Gdns. EH21 —7A **20**
Wemyss Pl. EH3
　　　　—2F **15** (2B **2**)
Wemyss Pl. EH32 —1A **20**

Wemyss Pl. M. EH3
　　　　—2F **15** (2B **2**)
W. Adam St. EH8
　　　　—4J **15** (5G **3**)
W. Annandale St. EH7 —7C **8**
W. Approach Rd. EH11 & EH3
　　　　—5B **14** (6A **2**)
Westbank. EH4 —6B **6**
Westbank Loan. EH15
　　　　—2G **17**
Westbank Pl. EH15 —2G **17**
Westbank St. EH15 —2G **17**
W. Barnton Ter. EH4 —2B **14**
West Bow. EH1 —4G **15**
W. Bowling Grn. St. EH6
　　　　—5D **8**
W. Brighton Cres. EH15
　　　　—3G **17**
W. Bryson Rd. EH11 —6D **14**
Westburn Av. EH14 —5E **22**
Westburn Gdns. EH14
　　　　—4E **22**
Westburn Gro. EH14 —4E **22**
Westburn Middlefield. EH14
　　　　—4E **22**
Westburn Pk. EH14 —4F **23**
W. Cairn Cres. EH26 —5B **34**
W. Caiystane Rd. EH10
　　　　—6E **24**
W. Carnethy Av. EH13
　　　　—7J **23**
W. Castle Rd. EH10 —6E **14**
W. Catherine Pl. EH12
　　　　—4C **14**
W. Coates. EH12 —4C **14**
W. College St. EH1
　　　　—4H **15** (5F **3**)
West Ct. EH4 —2A **14**
West Ct. EH16 —1E **26**
W. Craigs La. EH12 —5B **12**
W. Craigs Cres. EH12 —5B **12**
W. Craigs Ind. Est. EH12
　　　　—4B **12**
West Croft. EH28 —7C **10**
W. Cromwell St. EH6 —4E **8**
W. Crosscauseway. EH8
　　　　—5J **15** (7G **3**)
West End. EH2 —3F **15** (4A **2**)
W. End Pl. EH11 —5D **14**
Wester Broom Av. EH12
Wester Broom Dri. EH12
　　　　—6E **12**
Wester Broom Gdns. EH12
　　　　—6E **12**
Wester Broom Gro. EH12
　　　　—6E **12**
Wester Broom Pl. EH12
　　　　—5E **12**
Wester Broom Ter. EH12
　　　　—6E **12**
Wester Clo. EH6 —3C **8**
Wester Coates Av. EH12
　　　　—4C **14**
Wester Coates Gdns. EH12
　　　　—4C **14**
Wester Coates Pl. EH12
　　　　—3C **14**
Wester Coates Rd. EH12
　　　　—4C **14**
Wester Coates Ter. EH12
　　　　—4C **14**
Wester Drylaw Av. EH4
　　　　—7E **6**
Wester Drylaw Dri. EH4
　　　　—7D **6**
Wester Drylaw Pk. EH4 —7F **7**
Wester Drylaw Pl. EH4 —7E **6**
Wester Drylaw Row. EH4
　　　　—1A **14**
Wester Hailes Dri. EH14
　　　　—4F **23**
Wester Hailes Pk. EH14
　　　　—4G **23**
Wester Hailes Rd. EH11 &
　　　　EH14 —2E **22**
Wester Hill. EH10 —4C **24**
Western Corner. EH12
　　　　—4A **14**
Western Gdns. EH12 —4A **14**

Western Pl. EH12 —4A **14**
Western Ter. EH12 —4A **14**
Wester Row. EH14 —3A **22**
Wester Steil. EH10 —3C **24**
W. Ferryfield. EH5 —6J **7**
Westfield Av. EH11 —6A **14**
Westfield Ct. EH11 —6A **14**
Westfield Ct. EH22 —4D **32**
Westfield Gro. EH22 —4D **32**
Westfield Pk. EH22 —4D **32**
Westfield Rd. EH11 —6B **14**
Westfield St. EH11 —6B **14**
W. Fountain Pl. EH11
　　　　—5D **14**
Westgarth Av. EH13 —6K **23**
W. Gorgie Pk. EH14 —7A **14**
W. Gorgie Pl. EH14 —1A **24**
W. Grange Gdns. EH9
　　　　—7H **15**
W. Granton Cres. EH4 —4F **7**
W. Granton Dri. EH4 —5F **7**
W. Granton Grn. EH4 —5E **6**
W. Granton Rd. EH5 —4F **7**
W. Granton Row. EH4 —4F **7**
W. Granton Ter. EH4 —4F **7**
Westhall Gdns. EH10 —6F **15**
W. Harbour Rd. EH5 —3H **7**
W. Harbour Rd. EH32
　　　　—1A **20**
W. Holmes Gdns. EH21
　　　　—2D **18**
Westhouses Av. EH22
　　　　—1K **35**
Westhouses Dri. EH22
　　　　—1K **35**
Westhouses Rd. EH22
　　　　—1K **35**
Westhouses St. EH22 —1K **35**
W. Ingliston Cotts. EH28
　　　　—5E **10**
Westland Cotts. EH17 —7E **26**
W. Loan. EH32 —3D **20**
W. Loan Ct. EH32 —3D **20**
W. Lorimer Pl. EH32 —1F **21**
W. Mains Rd. EH9 —2J **25**
W. Maitland St. EH12 & EH3
　　　　—4E **14**
W. Mayfield. EH9 —7K **15**
W. Mill Ct. EH18 —4K **31**
W. Mill La. EH4 —3E **14**
W. Mill Rd. EH13 —6H **23**
W. Mill Wynd. EH18 —5K **31**
W. Montgomery Pl. EH7
　　　　—1K **15**
W. Newington Pl. EH9 —6J **15**
W. Nicolson St. EH8
　　　　—4J **15** (6G **3**)
W. Norton Pl. EH7
　　　　—2K **15** (1K **3**)
W. Park Pl. EH11 —5D **14**
W. Pier. EH5 —3H **7**
W. Pilton Av. EH4 —6F **7**
W. Pilton Bank. EH4 —5F **7**
W. Pilton Cres. EH4 —5E **6**
W. Pilton Crossway. EH4
　　　　—5F **7**
W. Pilton Dri. EH4 —5F **7**
W. Pilton Gdns. EH4 —5F **7**
W. Pilton Grn. EH4 —5F **7**
W. Pilton Gro. EH4 —5F **7**
W. Pilton Lea. EH4 —5F **7**
W. Pilton Loan. EH4 —5F **7**
W. Pilton Pk. EH4 —5F **7**
W. Pilton Pl. EH4 —5G **7**
W. Pilton Rise. EH4 —5F **7**
W. Pilton Rd. EH4 —1G **7**
W. Pilton St. EH4 —5F **7**
W. Pilton Ter. EH4 —5F **7**
W. Pilton View. EH4 —6F **7**
West Port. EH3 & EH1
　　　　—4G **15**
W. Powburn. EH9 —1J **25**
W. Preston St. EH8 —6J **15**
W. Register St. EH2
　　　　—2H **15** (2E **2**)

W. Register St. La. EH2
　　　　—2E **2**
W. Relugas Rd. EH9 —1H **25**
W. Richmond St. EH8
　　　　—4J **15** (6G **3**)
W. Savile Rd. EH16 —1K **25**
W. Savile Ter. EH9 —1J **25**
W. Seaside. EH32 —3D **20**
W. Shore Rd. EH5 —4E **6**
W. Silvermills La. EH3
　　　　—1F **15**
W. Stanhope Pl. EH12 —4C **14**
(off Stanhope Pl.)
West St. EH26 —7B **34**
W. Telferton. EH7 —2F **17**
West Ter. EH30 —5B **4**
(off High St. S. Queensferry)
W. Tollcross. EH3
　　　　—5F **15** (7B **2**)
W. Werberside. EH4 —6H **7**
W. Windygoul Gdns. EH33
　　　　—7G **21**
W. Winnelstrae. EH5 —6J **7**
W. Woods. EH4 —7H **7**
Wheatfield Pl. EH11 —6C **14**
Wheatfield Rd. EH11 —6B **14**
Wheatfield St. EH11 —6B **14**
Wheatfield Ter. EH11 —6B **14**
Wheatsheaf La. EH22 —2F **33**
Whin Pk. EH32 —1F **21**
Whin Pk. Ind. Est. EH32
　　　　—1F **21**
Whins Pl. EH15 —3G **17**
Whitecraig Av. EH21 —7G **19**
Whitecraig Cres. EH21
　　　　—7G **19**
Whitecraig Gdns. EH21
　　　　—7G **19**
Whitecraig Gdns. E. EH21
　　　　—7G **19**
Whitecraig Ter. EH21 —7G **19**
White Dales. EH10 —7G **25**
Whitehall Ct. EH4 —1K **13**
White Hart St. EH22 —2F **33**
(off Buccleuch St.)
Whitehead Gro. EH30 —6C **4**
Whitehill Av. EH21 —3C **18**
Whitehill Bus. Cen. EH22
　　　　—3K **33**
Whitehill Dri. EH22 —3J **33**
Whitehill Farm Rd. EH21
　　　　—4C **18**
Whitehill Gdns. EH21 —4C **18**
Whitehill Gro. EH22 —3J **33**
Whitehill Pl. EH24 —7F **35**
Whitehill Rd. EH15 & EH21
　　　　—7J **17**
Whitehill Rd. EH24 —7F **35**
Whitehill St. EH21 —7K **17**
Whitehorse Clo. EH8 —3J **3**
Whitehouse Loan. EH10 & EH9
　　　　—6F **15**
Whitehouse Rd. EH4 —7H **5**
Whitehouse Ter. EH9 —7G **15**
Whitelea Cres. EH14 —5E **28**
Whitelea Rd. EH14 —5E **28**
White Pk. EH11 —6C **14**
White's Clo. EH22 —2F **33**
Whitingford. EH6 —5C **8**
Whitson Cres. EH11 —6K **13**
Whitson Gro. EH11 —6K **13**
Whitson Pl. E. EH11 —6K **13**
Whitson Pl. W. EH11 —6K **13**
Whitson Rd. EH11 —6J **13**
Whitson Ter. EH11 —6K **13**
Whitson Wlk. EH11 —6J **13**
Whitson Way. EH11 —6K **13**
Whyte Pl. EH7 —2A **16**
Wilfred Ter. EH8 —2C **16**
Wilkieston Rd. EH28 —7A **10**
William Black Pl. EH30
　　　　—6C **4**
Williamfield Sq. EH15
　　　　—3G **17**
William Jameson Pl. EH15
　　　　—2G **17**
William St. EH3 —3E **14**
William St. La. N. E. EH3
　　　　—3E **14**

INDEX TO PLACES OF INTEREST

INDEX TO HOSPITALS

Astley Ainslie Hospital. —1G **25**

Beechmount Hocpital. —4K **13**
Bruntsfield Hospital. —6F **15**

Chalmers Hospital. —6D **2**
City Hospital. —4C **24**
Corstorphine Hospital. —5H **13**

Deaconess Hospital. —6H **3**
Douglas Ho. (Children's Hospital)
—7J **15**

Eastern General Hospital. —6J **9**
Edenhall Hospital. —4G **19**
Edinburgh Dental Hospital. —5E **2**
Elsie Inglis Memorial Maternity
Hospital.—2A **16**

Fairmile Nursing Home. —7H **25**

Gogarburn Hospital. —6K **11**

Leith Hospital. —5E **8**
Liberton Hospital. —6B **26**

Loanhead Hospital. —5G **31**

Murrayfield Hospital, The. —4J **13**

Northern General Hospital. —6H **7**

Princess Alexandra Eye Pavilion.
—7D **2**
Princess Margaret Rose Orthopaedic
Hospital. —7G **25**

Queensberry House Hospital. —3J **3**

Royal Edinburgh Hospital. —1E **24**
Royal Hospital for Sick Children.
—6H **15**
Royal Infirmary. —7E **2**
Royal Victoria Hospital. —1C **14**

Simpson Memorial Maternity Pavilion.
—7D **2**
Southfield Hospital. —5C **26**

Western General Hospital. —1C **14**